GÉOGRAPHIE

COURS ÉLÉMENTAIRE

aux maîtres

Le présent manuel a été établi avec la collaboration d'enseignants de tous les pays francophones groupés au sein de l'Institut Pédagogique Africain et Malgache : leur concours est la garantie de son exacte conformité aux besoins de vos élèves.

● Pour corriger l'une ou l'autre imperfection que vous pourriez être amenés à relever,

● pour que les manuels à paraître soient toujours en progrès sur les précédents,

faites part de vos remarques, de vos suggestions, de vos idées aux délégués de l'I.P.A.M. de votre pays, ou directement à : **I.P.A.M., Secrétariat général, 58, rue Jean-Bleuzen, 92178 Vanves Cedex.**

La photographie de couverture représente un marché à Abidjan, Côte d'Ivoire. (Ph. R. Michaud-Rapho.)

INSTITUT PÉDAGOGIQUE AFRICAIN ET MALGACHE

GÉOGRAPHIE

Cours élémentaire

Nouvelle édition

EDICEF

58, rue Jean-Bleuzen, 92178 VANVES

I.S.B.N. 2.850.69112.7

Ce nouvel ouvrage de l'*IPAM*, fait par des Africains pour des Africains, destiné aux élèves des *Cours Élémentaires* 1re *et* 2e *années* (ou des 3e et 4e années) des Écoles Primaires d'Afrique Noire est conforme aux grandes lignes des *Programmes officiels* des différents États.

CONFORME AU PROGRAMME

● Il s'inspire des *méthodes* les plus modernes de l'enseignement de la géographie. Il se propose d'initier l'enfant à « *l'observation et à la compréhension des grands faits géographiques et de leur vocabulaire usuel* ».

SELON LES MÉTHODES ACTIVES

Chaque fois que cela est possible « *les leçons sont fondées sur une observation attentive du milieu local* »; elles sont « *données dans la cour de l'école, ou en promenade, ou suivies d'observations ou d'exercices sur le terrain* ». Pour compléter l'observation ou pour mieux la préciser, l'ouvrage est illustré de *figures* et de *photographies* que les auteurs ont voulues grandes, claires et caractéristiques.

OBSERVER

L'enfant lui-même doit prendre une part active à l'enseignement de la géographie : *observer, noter ses observations, en rendre compte ; répondre à des questions dirigées ; dessiner ; construire, avec les matériaux locaux, des maquettes de sa maison, de son école, de son village. L'observation*, à la verticale, de ces maquettes lui suggérera l'idée de la *représentation cartographique* et le préparera à la lecture du *plan* et de la *carte*.

EXPLIQUER

● Chaque leçon est précédée de *directives pour l'observation* du milieu ou des illustrations. Le texte de la *leçon*, simple, clair, vivant, doit être lu et expliqué. Des *questions* et *exercices* permettent de préciser les notions expliquées au cours de la leçon et, parfois, de redresser certaines erreurs.

Des *résumés* brefs et concis fixent les notions et les définitions à *apprendre par cœur*.

RETENIR

● Sans doute ce petit ouvrage ne répondra-t-il pas encore exactement à tous les besoins locaux, dans une région aussi vaste et aussi variée que l'Afrique Noire. Il appartient au maître de choisir ce qui convient particulièrement à ses élèves, *d'adapter* et d'expliquer ce qu'ils ne peuvent comprendre.

● Sans doute aussi toutes les leçons ne conviennent-elles pas, telles quelles, à toutes les classes. Pour faciliter le travail du maître, des *dispositions typographiques* spéciales différencient ce que doivent apprendre les élèves de C.E. 1 (ou de 3e année) des compléments en petits caractères et placés en retrait, réservés à ceux du C.E. 2 (ou de 4e année). De même dans *les questions et exercices*, les textes en retrait sont destinés aux élèves du C.E. 2.

UTILISABLE PENDANT LES 2 ANNÉES DE COURS ÉLÉMENTAIRE

Lorsqu'il l'estimera nécessaire, le maître pourra répartir la matière de la leçon en 2 ou 3 séances.

En toute occasion *le maître adaptera son enseignement* au niveau de ses élèves.

● Ce que l'IPAM a voulu, une fois de plus, c'est offrir à tous un livre *clair, simple, concret* et *vivant*, un auxiliaire précieux pour les maîtres africains et un agréable compagnon pour leurs petits écoliers.

LES QUATRE POINTS CARDINAUX

Photo Archives Hachette.

Fig. 1 - C'est le matin, de très bonne heure ; le soleil apparaît derrière les îles de Loos (Guinée).

OBSERVONS

Le soleil se lève-t-il toujours au même endroit? En nous plaçant au même endroit de la cour, notons chaque jour le point où il se lève, puis le point où il se couche.

Regardons une **boussole** *(figure 2)* Comment est-elle faite? Notons dans quelle direction se tourne l'aiguille.

La nuit, avec notre maître, regardons les étoiles dans le ciel et apprenons à les reconnaître, à retrouver l'**Étoile polaire** *(figure 4)* ou la **Croix du Sud.**

LEÇON

Le matin, le soleil se lève toujours au même endroit que l'on appelle l'**Est** ou le **Levant.** Le soir, il se couche à l'**Ouest** que l'on appelle aussi le **Couchant.** A midi, le soleil se trouve bien haut dans le ciel, presque au-dessus de nos têtes. Quand je regarde le soleil se lever, j'ai l'**Est** devant moi et l'**Ouest** derrière moi. J'ai le **Sud** à ma droite et le **Nord** à ma gauche.

L'**Est**, l'**Ouest**, le **Nord** et le **Sud** sont les quatre **points cardinaux.**

S'orienter c'est chercher où sont les quatre points cardinaux. Le jour il est facile de s'orienter à l'aide du soleil.

La nuit, nous ne voyons plus le soleil.

Fig. 2 - Une boussole.

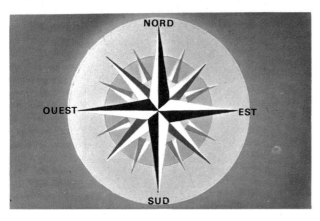

Fig. 3 - Une rose des vents.

Fig. 4 - Je cherche l'Étoile polaire.

Des étoiles brillent dans le ciel. L'une d'elles, l'**Étoile polaire,** nous indique le **Nord.**

Pour trouver l'**Étoile polaire,** cherchons d'abord la **Grande Ourse** ou le **Grand Chariot** que nous montre la *figure 4.* En suivant la direction de ses 2 dernières étoiles nous trouvons l'**Étoile polaire.** Cherchons, à l'opposé, la **Croix du Sud,** dans l'hémisphère sud.

Le jour et la nuit, lorsque le ciel est couvert de nuages, nous ne voyons ni le soleil ni les étoiles. Nous pouvons nous orienter à l'aide d'une **boussole.** Une **boussole** est une aiguille aimantée qui se tourne toujours vers le **Nord.** Lorsque j'ai trouvé le **Nord** à l'aide de la boussole, il m'est ensuite facile de retrouver les trois autres points cardinaux.

QUESTIONS ET EXERCICES

A l'aide du soleil, le matin ou le soir, trouvons l'Est ou l'Ouest. Trouvons ensuite le Nord et le Sud. Vérifions les points ainsi trouvés avec la boussole.

De nuit, apprenons à reconnaître la Grande Ourse puis à trouver l'Étoile polaire ou la Croix du Sud.

Dessinons une boussole. Dessinons et colorions une « rose des vents » (figure 3).

RÉSUMÉ

S'orienter, c'est rechercher les quatre points cardinaux. Les quatre points cardinaux sont : l'Est, le Sud, l'Ouest et le Nord.

Je peux m'orienter le jour à l'aide du soleil, la nuit à l'aide de l'Étoile polaire ou de la Croix du Sud, de jour et de nuit à l'aide d'une boussole.

2 LE PLAN DE MA MAISON

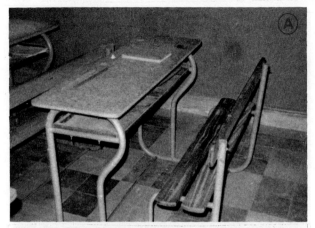

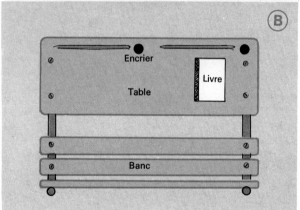

Fig. 1 - La table, le livre et l'encrier.

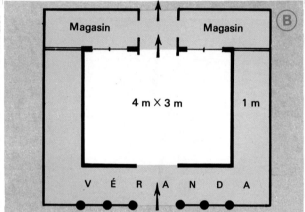

Fig. 2 - Une maison de mon village.

OBSERVONS

Autour de nous : Regardons bien, en nous plaçant au-dessus d'eux, notre livre fermé, un encrier, une table-banc.
Les documents : La *figure 2 A* est la photographie de la maison d'un camarade. Montrons la porte, les murs, la véranda. Sur l'image *(figure 2 B)* recherchons la porte, les murs, et la véranda de la maison.
La *figure 3* est la photographie d'une salle de classe comme la nôtre. Montrons la porte, le tableau noir, le bureau du maître et les tables des élèves. Recherchons-les sur la *figure 4.*

LEÇON

Les dessins de notre livre, de notre encrier, de notre table *(figure 1 B)*, représentent ces objets vus de dessus. Ce sont les **plans** de ces objets.

Le **plan** du livre est un rectangle. Celui de l'encrier est un rond, celui de la table-banc est fait de plusieurs rectangles côte à côte.

Ces **plans** sont beaucoup plus petits que les objets qu'ils représentent.

Je fais le **plan de la maison** de mon camarade *(figure 2 B)*. Je la dessine comme si je la voyais de très haut et si on avait enlevé le toit.

8

Fig. 3 - Photographie de la salle de classe.

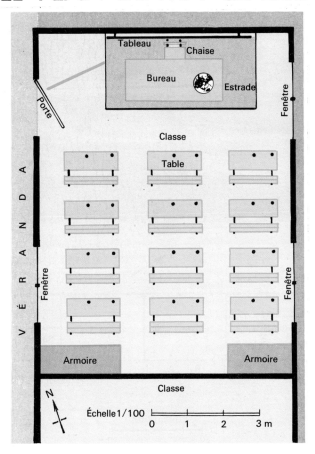

Fig. 4 - Le plan de la salle de classe.

Je trace les murs et j'indique la porte et la véranda. Le **plan de la maison** est bien plus petit que la maison.

La *figure 4* est le **plan de la classe** dessiné d'après la photographie *(figure 3)*. On y retrouve comme sur la photographie, les murs, la porte, les fenêtres, le tableau noir, le bureau du maître et 3 rangées de tables-bancs.

Essayons de dessiner le **plan** de notre classe.

Ce dessin est plus petit que la classe. La classe a 9 m de long et 7 m de large. Sur le plan elle a 9 cm de long et 7 cm de large. 1 cm du plan représente 1 m de la classe.

Sur le **plan,** on a indiqué le **Nord** à l'aide d'une flèche. On dit que le plan est **orienté.**

QUESTIONS ET EXERCICES

Refaisons très soigneusement, avec une règle et un compas, les plans du livre, de l'encrier et de la table-banc.
Faisons le plan d'une maison du village.

Mesurons notre classe avant d'en faire le plan. 1 cm (ou 1 carreau de notre cahier) représentera 1 m de notre classe. Traçons les murs avec les portes et les fenêtres. Plaçons le tableau noir, le bureau du maître, l'armoire, puis les tables des élèves.
Orientons le plan en y indiquant le Nord.

RÉSUMÉ

Le plan d'un objet est le dessin de cet objet vu de dessus. Le plan est plus petit que l'objet. Sur un plan, une flèche nous montre où se trouve le Nord. On dit que le plan est orienté.

3 LE PLAN DE L'ÉCOLE ET DE MON VILLAGE

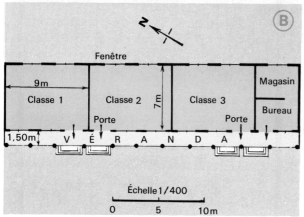

Fig. 1 - Une école de brousse.

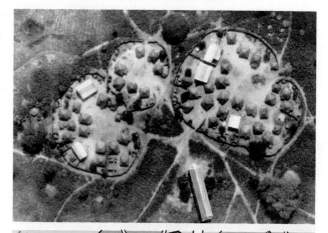

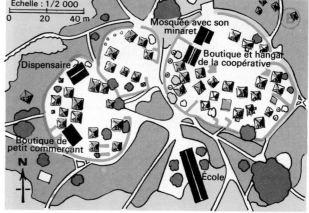

Fig. 2 - Un village.

OBSERVONS

La *figure 1 A* est la **photographie** d'une petite école de village et la *figure 1 B* est le **plan** de cette école. Cherchons sur ces 2 figures, la cour, la véranda, les classes et le bureau du directeur.

La *figure 2 A* est la **photographie** prise d'avion, d'un petit village comme le nôtre. La *figure 2 B* est le **plan** de ce village. Cherchons les routes, la place du village, l'école et le dispensaire.

La *figure 4* est le **plan** du quartier d'une ville que nous voyons, photographiée d'avion, sur la *figure 3*.

LEÇON

La *figure 1 A* est la *photographie* d'une petite école de village. On y voit la cour avec quelques arbres, les classes et le bureau du directeur. La *figure 1 B* est le **plan** de cette école. On y trouve la cour, la véranda, les 3 classes et le bureau du directeur.

Faisons le plan de notre école. Traçons les limites de la cour. Plaçons les classes, la véranda, les logements des maîtres. Orientons notre plan.

La *figure 2 A* est la photographie, prise d'avion, d'un petit village d'Afrique. Nous y trouvons les routes, la place du village, l'école,

Fig. 3 - Photographie aérienne d'un quartier
d'une grande ville.

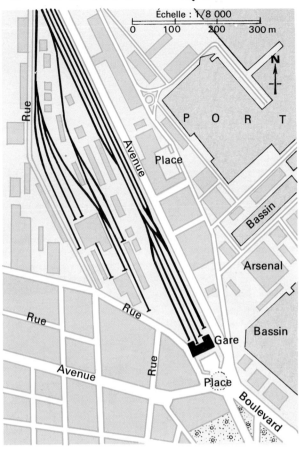

Fig. 4 - Le plan de ce quartier.

le dispensaire, les maisons et même les champs et les arbres.

Tous ces lieux se retrouvent sur la *figure 2 B* qui est le **plan de ce village,** fait d'après la photographie.

De la même façon, nous retrouvons sur la *figure 4,* qui est le **plan d'un quartier** d'une grande ville d'Afrique, les rues, les bâtiments et la gare que l'on voit sur la photographie de ce quartier *(figure 3).* Nous y retrouvons aussi le port avec les bassins et les quais.

Le **plan du village** et le **plan du quartier** sont bien plus petits que le village ou le quartier. L'école sur la *figure 2 B* est bien plus petite encore qu'elle n'était sur la *figure 1 B.*

QUESTIONS ET EXERCICES

Apprenons à faire le plan de notre école.

Apprenons à faire le plan de notre village ou de notre quartier. Orientons ces plans.

Traçons au crayon le chemin que nous suivons chaque matin pour venir à l'école, puis pour aller de l'école au dispensaire.

RÉSUMÉ

Le plan de l'école est le dessin de l'école vue de dessus. Le plan de mon village ou de mon quartier est le dessin, très simplifié, de ses routes ou de ses rues, de ses bâtiments. Le plan est beaucoup plus petit que l'école, que mon village ou que mon quartier.

LA CAMPAGNE AUTOUR DE MON VILLAGE

Fig. 1 - Un pays plat.

OBSERVONS

Autour de nous : Montons au point le plus élevé de notre village et regardons autour de nous. Que voyons-nous ? Le pays est-il plat ? A-t-il des bosses ? Les routes sont-elles plates et droites ? Ont-elles beaucoup de tournants ?

Les documents : La *figure 1* nous montre un pays plat et la *figure 2* représente, au contraire, un pays bosselé. Suivons du doigt, sur ces gravures, la ligne où le ciel semble toucher la terre.

LEÇON

Nous voici, avec notre maître, au point le plus élevé de notre village. Regardons autour de nous.

Nous voyons, à nos pieds, l'école, la mosquée et l'église, les maisons et les routes qui conduisent aux villages voisins.

Là-bas, au loin et de tous les côtés, la terre semble finir. Le ciel semble la toucher. La ligne qui marque cet endroit où le ciel semble toucher la terre s'appelle la **ligne d'horizon.**

Lorsque le pays est plat, comme sur la *figure 1*, **l'horizon** est presque une ligne droite. Si, au contraire, comme sur la *figure 2*, la campagne

Fig. 2 - Un pays de collines.

est bosselée, la **ligne d'horizon** est une ligne brisée.

La *figure 1* représente un **pays plat.** Les champs s'étendent à perte de vue. Les routes sont plates et droites. Un cycliste y roule facilement.

La *figure 2* nous montre, au contraire, un pays tout bosselé. Les parties plates y sont rares. Les routes montent et descendent sans cesse. Elles ont de nombreux virages. Un cycliste a beaucoup de mal à rouler. Il doit souvent descendre de machine et monter les côtes à pied.

Les étendues plates, les creux et les bosses du terrain forment le **relief** d'une région.

QUESTIONS ET EXERCICES

Notre région est-elle plate ou accidentée ? Les routes montent-elles ou descendent-elles pour aller vers les villages voisins ?

Du point le plus haut de notre village, regardons l'horizon autour de nous. La ligne d'horizon est-elle une ligne droite ou une ligne brisée ? Essayons de la dessiner.

RÉSUMÉ

L'horizon est la ligne où le ciel semble toucher la terre. Dans un pays plat, la ligne d'horizon est une ligne droite. Dans un pays bosselé, la ligne d'horizon est une ligne brisée. Les étendues plates, les creux et les bosses du terrain forment le relief d'une région.

5 PLAINES ET PLATEAUX

Fig. 1 - Plaine en Guinée, traversée par une rivière qui se jette dans le Niger.
Vue prise d'un avion.

OBSERVONS

Autour de nous : Notre pays est-il plat ? Est-il accidenté et y voit-on des bosses de terrain ? Sont-elles grandes ou petites ?

Les documents : La *figure 1* est celle d'un pays plat. Comment y sont les routes ? Comment y coulent les rivières ?

La *figure 2* nous montre un pays accidenté. Suivons du doigt la ligne d'horizon. Comment est-elle ? Voyons-nous des routes, des villages, des cultures sur cette gravure ?

LEÇON

Sur la *figure 1*, nous voyons une région plate qui s'étend à perte de vue, jusqu'à l'horizon. La ligne d'horizon est une ligne droite.
Cette région plate s'appelle une **plaine.** Les routes y sont toutes droites. La rivière coule très lentement en décrivant des courbes.

La terre est facile à cultiver. Une plaine est souvent une région de riches cultures.

Parfois le sol s'élève petit à petit et forme des petites bosses. Ces petites bosses, de faible hauteur, ont leur sommet arrondi. On les appelle des **collines.** Sur leurs pentes, on voit quelques cultures. Parfois, un village se dresse au sommet de la colline.

Photo Fouquer/AAA-Photo.

Fig. 2 - Le Kilimandjaro (Tanzanie), montagne haute de 5 900 m, dresse, au-dessus des nuages, son sommet couvert de neige.

Quelquefois, après avoir monté une pente, nous arrivons sur une nouvelle étendue plate. Cette plaine élevée est un **plateau.**

La *figure 2* nous montre une région très haute et très accidentée. C'est une **montagne** d'Afrique. Il est très difficile d'en atteindre le sommet car les côtés sont très en pente. Il y a peu de routes dans les montagnes et aussi peu de villages.

> Au pied de la montagne, il y a des cultures. Plus haut, il y a encore quelques arbres et des pâturages. Au sommet, il ne pousse plus rien.

Certaines hautes montagnes d'Afrique ont leur sommet couvert de neige. Ces neiges ne fondent jamais. On les appelle des **neiges éternelles.**

QUESTIONS ET EXERCICES

Y a-t-il des plaines autour de notre village ? Comment sont les routes dans ces plaines ? Comment y coulent les rivières ? Y a-t-il des montagnes autour de notre village ? Comment les nomme-t-on ?

Trouve-t-on des cultures dans ces montagnes ? Lesquelles ? Y trouve-t-on beaucoup de villages ? Lesquels ?

Sur la carte de notre pays, apprenons à montrer les plaines, les collines, les plateaux et, s'il y en a, les montagnes.

RÉSUMÉ

Une plaine est une grande étendue de terrain plat.
Une colline est une petite élévation de terrain.
Un plateau est une plaine élevée.
Les montagnes sont, comme les collines, des élévations de terrain ; mais elles sont beaucoup plus hautes.

DU PLAN A LA CARTE

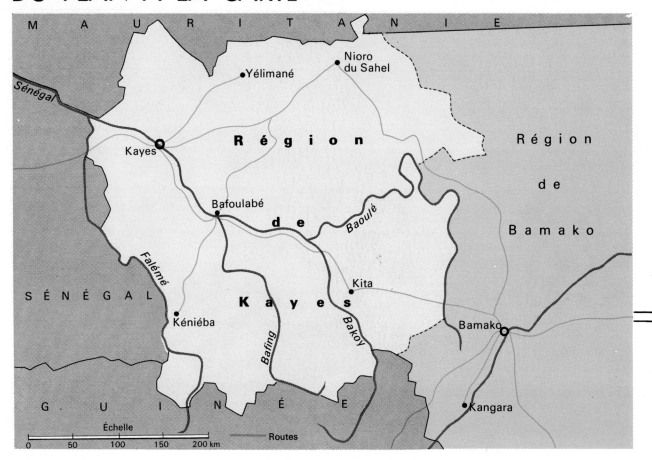

Fig. 1 - La carte de la région de Kayes, dans la République du Mali.

OBSERVONS

Reprenons, dans les leçons précédentes (2 et 3), le plan de la classe et ceux de l'école et du village. La classe dessinée sur la *figure 4* de la *page 9* apparaît-elle aussi grande sur le plan de l'école *(figure 1 B, page 10)* ? La voit-on sur le plan du village *(figure 2, p. 10)* ou du quartier ?

Regardons maintenant les *figures 1* et *2*, de cette leçon 6.

Que représente la *figure 1* ? Y voyons-nous notre petit village ? Que représente la *figure 2* ? Montrons du doigt sur la *figure 2* la région que nous avons vue sur la *figure 1*.

LEÇON

Nous avons fait, au cours des *leçons 2 et 3*, les **plans** de notre **classe,** de notre **école,** puis de notre **village** ou de notre **quartier.** Nous pouvons aussi faire le plan de notre département, de notre région ou de notre État, qui sont beaucoup plus étendus. Un tel plan, qui représente une grande surface s'appelle une **carte.**

Regardons les *cartes 1 et 2* qui représentent une région d'Afrique : la **région de Kayes,** et un pays : le **Mali.**

Nous ne pouvons plus représenter une école ou des maisons sur la carte de la région.

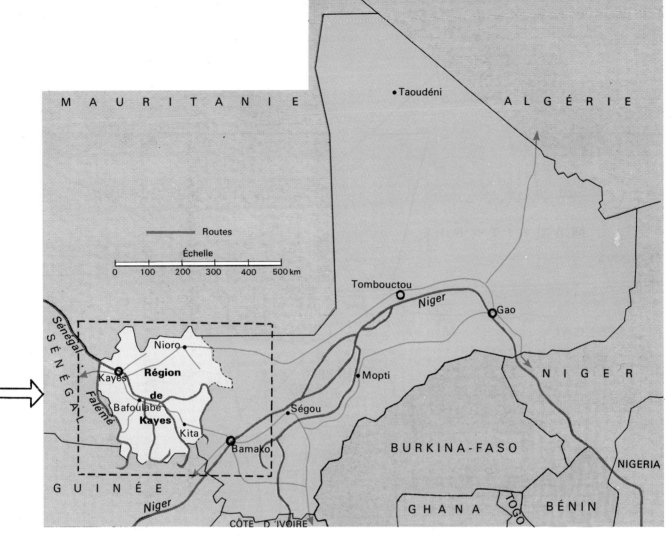

Fig. 2 - La carte du Mali.

Elles seraient beaucoup trop petites. Les villages les plus importants sont représentés par un point et les villes par un cercle.

Sur la *carte 2* qui représente l'État du **Mali,** on ne voit plus les villages, mais seulement les villes les plus importantes.

Sur une **carte,** nous n'indiquons pas seulement les villes. Nous y traçons aussi les grandes routes, les lignes de chemin de fer et les plus grandes rivières.

On y indique parfois, avec des couleurs différentes les plaines, les collines et les montagnes. Très souvent, les plaines sont indiquées en vert, les collines en marron clair et les montagnes en marron plus foncé.

QUESTIONS ET EXERCICES

Apprenons à reconnaître sur les cartes 1 et 2 une grande ville, une petite ville, une rivière, une route.

   Montrons, sur la grande carte, que le maître a fixée au mur, des régions de plaines, des collines, des montagnes.

Apprenons à faire la carte de notre région, puis de notre pays.
Apprenons à trouver notre pays et les pays voisins sur la carte de l'Afrique Noire (p. 18).

RÉSUMÉ

Sur mon livre, ma région et mon pays sont représentés par une carte. Sur une carte, je ne vois plus les petits villages mais seulement les villes les plus importantes. J'y vois aussi les routes, les lignes de chemin de fer et les rivières.
Je peux y reconnaître les plaines, les collines et les montagnes.

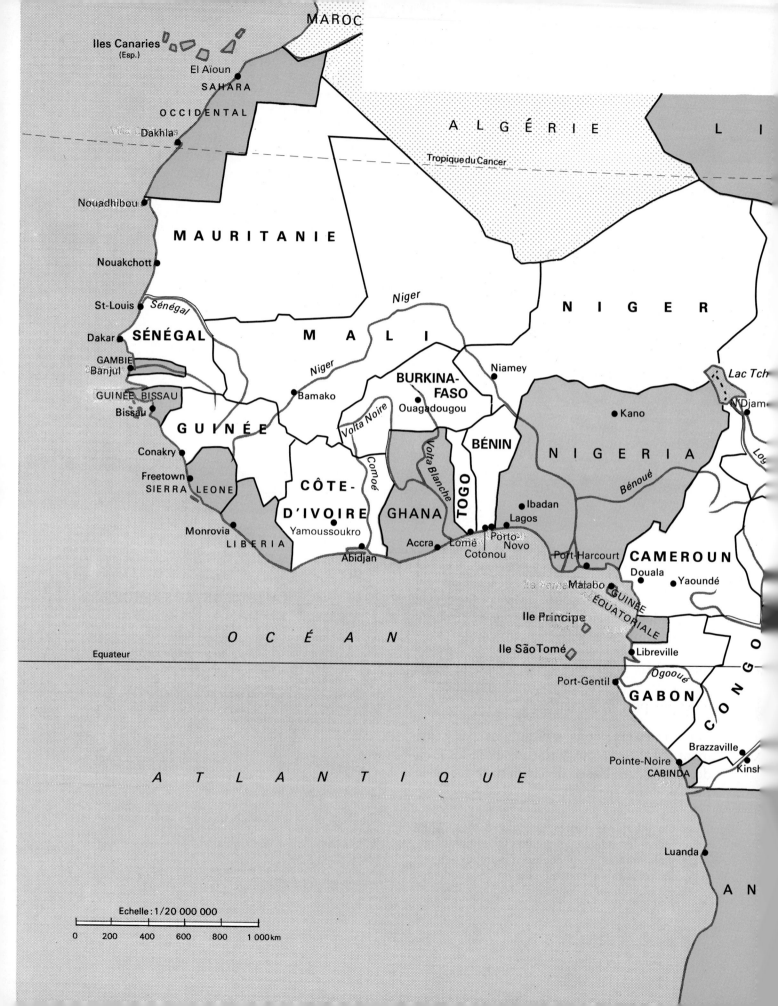

OBSERVONS

Comme nous avons fait les plans de notre école, de notre village, nous apprendrons, plus tard, à faire aussi la carte de notre département, de notre pays et même celle de toute l'Afrique Noire.

Sur cette carte, on ne place plus les maisons ni les villages, ni les petites villes : ils sont beaucoup trop petits. Les grandes villes de chaque pays sont représentées par un point noir. Nous y voyons encore les grandes rivières et tous les pays de l'Afrique Noire.

QUESTIONS ET EXERCICES

Nous n'apprendrons pas à faire la carte de l'Afrique Noire tout seuls; c'est beaucoup trop difficile.
Apprenons d'abord à y reconnaître notre pays, puis tous les pays voisins.

Sur une carte muette que notre maître aura faite au tableau, apprenons à situer les différents pays de l'Afrique Noire
Ensuite, avec un camarade, jouons aux devinettes :
« Montre-moi le Mali, le Zaïre, le Nigeria... »,
puis à son tour, mon camarade me montre un pays et me demande : « Qu'est-ce que c'est ? » Je réponds :
« C'est le Sénégal. » ... et nous continuons. Ce n'est pas facile, mais c'est très amusant. Nous apprenons, en jouant, beaucoup de choses utiles.

8 LA TERRE EST RONDE

Photo Holmès-Lebel.

Fig. 1 - L'Afrique photographiée d'un satellite artificiel volant à 300 kilomètres de hauteur.

OBSERVONS

Autour de nous : Un avion passe au-dessus de nos têtes. Il s'éloigne et semble descendre. Il disparaît à l'horizon.

Les documents : La *figure 1* est une photographie de la terre prise de très haut. Comment est son contour ? La *figure 2* nous explique comment, au bord de la mer, nous voyons un bateau qui s'avance vers nous. Nous voyons d'abord la fumée, puis les cheminées, puis tout le bateau. Pourquoi ?

LEÇON

La photographie de la terre, prise de très haut *(figure 1)*, nous montre que la surface de la terre est courbe. Le bateau que nous voyons approcher *(figure 2)*, l'avion qui nous survole puis disparaît derrière l'horizon, nous montrent que **la terre est ronde.**

Dans nos classes, pour montrer aux petits écoliers que la terre est ronde, on la représente par un **globe terrestre.** Ce globe tourne autour d'un axe qui le traverse de haut en bas.

Le point de la terre situé le plus au Nord s'appelle le **pôle Nord.** Le point situé le plus au Sud s'appelle le **pôle Sud.**

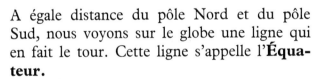

Fig. 2 - La terre est ronde.

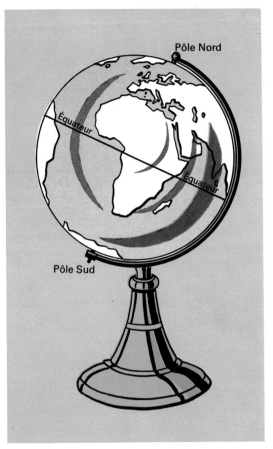

Fig. 3 - Un globe terrestre.

A égale distance du pôle Nord et du pôle Sud, nous voyons sur le globe une ligne qui en fait le tour. Cette ligne s'appelle l'**Équateur.**

Nous croyons que le soleil tourne autour de la terre. C'est une erreur. Le soleil ne bouge pas et c'est la terre qui tourne.

Fermons les volets et éclairons le globe avec une bougie : une moitié du globe est éclairée et l'autre moitié est dans l'ombre.
De la même manière, le soleil éclaire la terre. Quand il fait jour pour une moitié de la terre, il fait nuit pour l'autre moitié. Mais la terre tourne comme le globe. C'est parce que la terre tourne sur elle-même en 24 heures, sans jamais s'arrêter, que le jour et la nuit se succèdent.

QUESTIONS ET EXERCICES

Quelle est la forme de la terre ? Sur le globe terrestre montrons le pôle Nord, le pôle Sud. Cherchons l'Équateur et suivons-le avec le doigt.
Dessinons le globe terrestre. Indiquons le pôle Nord, le pôle Sud et l'Équateur.

Recommençons tout seuls, avec le globe terrestre et la bougie, l'expérience que le maître nous a faite.

RÉSUMÉ

La terre est ronde. Son point le plus au Nord s'appelle le pôle Nord. Son point le plus au Sud est le pôle Sud. L'Équateur est une ligne qui se trouve à égale distance des deux pôles.
La terre tourne sur elle-même en 24 heures. C'est pour cela que le jour et la nuit se succèdent.

9 LE JOUR

Photo Pierre/AAA-Photo.

Fig. 1 - Le soleil se couche au-dessus du fleuve Sénégal.

OBSERVONS

Autour de nous : Le soleil se lève. Où le voyons-nous apparaître ? A quel moment est-il le plus haut ? A quel moment fait-il le plus chaud ? Où se couche le soleil ? Il fait nuit. Que voyons-nous dans le ciel ? La lune a-t-elle toujours la même forme ?

Les documents : Sur la *figure 1* où se trouve le soleil. Est-il haut au-dessus de l'horizon ?
Sur la *figure 2*, nous voyons la marche du soleil dans le ciel. Montrons-le à son lever, à 9 heures, à midi, à 3 heures, le soir, à son coucher.

LEÇON

Le matin, lorsqu'on se lève de bonne heure, on voit le ciel s'éclaircir vers l'**Est.** Le soleil, tout rond, apparaît à l'horizon puis monte dans le ciel.
Les paysans et les ouvriers vont au travail. Les écoliers partent pour l'école.

> Il fait frais, puis, à mesure que le soleil monte dans le ciel, il fait de plus en plus chaud.

A midi, le soleil brille juste au-dessus de nos têtes.

> Il fait bien trop chaud pour travailler. Les hommes et les bêtes se reposent à l'ombre. C'est l'heure du repos et de la sieste.

Plus tard, le soleil redescend et le travail

Fig. 2 - La marche du soleil dans le ciel.

recommence. Il est bientôt à l'**Ouest** et disparaît derrière l'horizon. Le travail est fini. Hommes et bêtes rentrent au village. Les écoliers quittent l'école. Il fait de plus en plus sombre puis, tout d'un coup, il fait **nuit.**

Il fait plus froid. Dans les maisons, les feux de bois et les lampes s'allument.

Dans le ciel, les **étoiles** brillent et la **lune** se lève. Ce sera bientôt l'heure de dormir.

Mais, en Afrique, c'est aussi l'heure des contes et l'heure de la danse. Le tam-tam et le balafon résonnent.

Partout, sur toute la terre, la succession du jour et de la nuit règle la vie des hommes.

QUESTIONS ET EXERCICES

Notons le point de l'horizon où le soleil se lève et le point où il se couche.
Chaque jour, notons l'heure du lever du soleil et celle de son coucher.
Calculons la durée du jour et la durée de la nuit.
Dessinons les différentes formes de la lune. Combien se passe-t-il de jours entre chacune de ces formes ?

RÉSUMÉ

Le soleil se lève à l'Est, monte dans le ciel, puis redescend et se couche à l'Ouest.
Le jour, il éclaire et réchauffe la terre. C'est le moment où les hommes travaillent.
Lorsque le soleil se couche, il fait nuit. C'est, pour les hommes, le moment de se reposer.

10 LE CALENDRIER

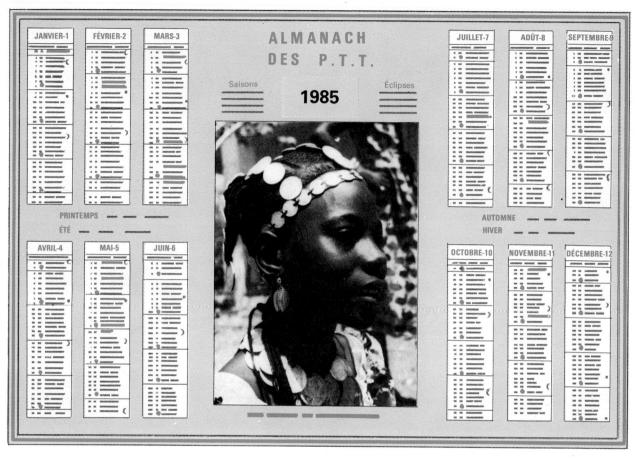

Fig. 1 - Un calendrier annuel.

OBSERVONS

Autour de nous: Le jour et la nuit se succèdent sans jamais s'arrêter. Chaque matin le maître change la date au tableau. Quelle est la date d'aujourd'hui? Nous avons des jours de classe. Lesquels? Nous avons des jours de vacances. Lesquels?

Quel est le jour du marché? le jour de la prière?

Les documents : Ils représentent des calendriers. Cherchons-y les mois, les jours, les saisons, la date.

LEÇON

Le jour et la nuit se succèdent sans jamais s'arrêter et, chaque matin, le maître écrit la **date** au tableau. Par exemple : **vendredi 22 novembre 1985**. Il indique d'abord le **jour**. Les jours se nomment : **lundi, mardi, mercredi, jeudi, vendredi, samedi** et **dimanche**. Le maître inscrit ensuite un **nombre** entre **1** et **31**.

Il y a 30 ou 31 jours dans un mois. Seul le mois de février a 28 ou 29 jours.

Le nom du **mois** vient après. Il y a **12 mois** dans une année : **janvier, février, mars, avril, mai, juin, juillet, août, septembre, octobre, novembre, décembre.**

OCTOBRE-10	NOVEMBRE-11	DÉCEMBRE-12
O 5 h 51 à 17 h 29	O 6 h 39 à 16 h 29	O 7 h 24 à 15 h 55
1 M SᵉTh.del'E.J.	1 V TOUSSAINT	1 D Avent
2 M S. Léger	2 S Défunts	2 L SᵉViviane
3 J S. Gérard	3 D S. Hubert	3 M S. Xavier
4 V S. Fr. d'Assise		4 M SᵉBarbara
5 S SᵉFleur	4 L S. Charles	5 J S. Gérald
6 D S. Bruno	5 M SᵉSylvie	6 V S. Nicolas
	6 M SᵉBertille	7 S S. Ambroise
7 L S. Serge	7 J SᵉCarine	8 D Imm. Concept.
8 M SᵉPélagie	8 V S. Geoffroy	
9 M S. Denis	9 S S. Théodore	9 L S. P. Fourier
10 J S. Ghislain	10 D S. Léon	10 M S. Romaric
11 V S. Firmin		11 M S. Daniel
12 S S. Wilfried	11 L ARMISTICE 1918	12 J SᵉJeanneF.C.
13 D S. Géraud	12 M S. Christian	13 V SᵉLucie
	13 M S. Brice	14 S SᵉOdile
14 L S. Juste	14 J S. Sidoine	15 D SᵉNinon
15 M SᵉTh. d'Avila	15 V S. Albert	
16 M SᵉEdwige	16 S SᵉMarguerite	16 L SᵉAlice
17 J S. Baudouin	17 D SᵉElisabeth	17 M S. Gaël
18 V S. Luc		18 M S. Gatien
19 S S. René	18 L SᵉAude	19 J S. Urbain
20 D SᵉAdeline	19 M S. Tanguy	20 V S. Abraham
	20 M S. Edmond	21 S HIVER
21 L SᵉCéline	21 J Prés. de Marie	22 D SᵉFr-Xavière
22 M SᵉElodie	22 V SᵉCécile	
23 M S. Jean de C.	23 S S. Clément	23 L S. Armand
24 J S. Florentin	24 D SᵉFlora	24 M SᵉAdèle
25 V S. Crépin		25 M NOËL
26 S S. Dimitri	25 L SᵉCatherine L.	26 J S. Etienne
27 D SᵉEmeline	26 M SᵉDelphine	27 V S. Jean
	27 M S. Séverin	28 S SS. Innocents
28 L SS.Sim.,Jude	28 J S. Jacq.delaM.	29 D S. David
29 M S. Narcisse	29 V S. Saturnin	
30 M S. Bienvenue	30 S S. André	30 L S. Roger
31 J S. Quentin		31 M S. Sylvestre
	Hiver, 22 Décembre	

Fig. 2 - Un calendrier trimestriel.

NOVEMBRE - 11

dimanche		3	10	17	24
lundi		4	11	18	25
mardi		5	12	19	26
mercredi		6	13	20	27
jeudi		7	14	21	28
vendredi	1	8	15	22	29
samedi	2	9	16	23	30

Fig. 3 - Un calendrier mensuel.

Fig. 4 - Un calendrier perpétuel.

1985 est le nom de l'**année.** Nous sommes en 1985. L'année dernière nous étions en 1984. L'année prochaine nous serons en 1986. Dans une **année,** il y a **12 mois** ou **52 semaines** ou **365 jours.** L'année commence le 1ᵉʳ janvier et se termine le 31 décembre.

Pour connaître la date exacte, nous nous servons d'un **calendrier.** Nous avons dans notre classe un calendrier des postes comme celui de la *figure 1.* Notre maître a un calendrier dont il arrache une feuille chaque jour. D'autres calendriers ont une feuille pour trois mois *(figure 2)* ou pour chaque mois *(figure 3).*

Ces calendriers nous indiquent, avec les dates, le début de chaque saison.

QUESTIONS ET EXERCICES

Quelle est la date d'aujourd'hui ? Quelle est votre date de naissance ? la date de la rentrée des classes ? celle du départ en vacances ?

Faisons un calendrier perpétuel. Combien ferons-nous d'étiquettes pour les jours ? Écrivons en rouge les jours de congé et en noir les jours de classe. Combien nous faudra-t-il d'étiquettes pour les mois ? pour la date ?

RÉSUMÉ

7 jours : lundi, mardi, mercredi, jeudi, vendredi, samedi et dimanche font une semaine.
Dans un mois, il y a 30 ou 31 jours. Le mois de février a seulement 28 ou 29 jours.
Les 12 mois : janvier, février, mars, avril, mai, juin, juillet, août, septembre, octobre, novembre et décembre forment une année. Dans une année, il y a 12 mois ou 52 semaines ou 365 jours.

11 LE TEMPS QU'IL FAIT : LE VENT

Photo Naud/AAA-Photo.

Fig. 1 - Venant de la mer, le vent agite les palmes des cocotiers.

OBSERVONS

Autour de nous : Y a-t-il du vent ce matin ? A quoi le voyons-nous ? Regardons le drapeau, les brins d'herbe, les feuilles, les branches des arbres. Bougent-ils ?

De quelle direction souffle le vent aujourd'hui ? De quelle direction souffle-t-il en saison sèche ? en saison des pluies ?

La photographie : Regardons les palmes des cocotiers de la *figure 1*. Comment sont-elles ? Pourquoi ?

LEÇON

Agitons notre boubou, notre livre de géographie : la feuille de papier posée sur la table s'envole ; nous avons fait du **vent.** Le vent, c'est de l'air qui se déplace. Le vent fait flotter le drapeau de l'école. Il fait bouger les feuilles et les branches des arbres *(figure 1)*. Quand il souffle fort il peut même incliner les plus grosses branches.

Parfois le vent est très fort. Il souffle en **tempête.** Il soulève le sable, déracine les arbres et renverse les cases.

En **saison sèche, l'harmattan** est chaud et sec. Il brûle tout sur son passage. Il fait gercer nos lèvres et ternir notre peau.

26

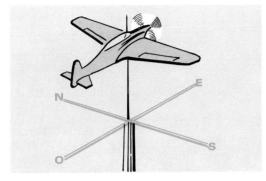

Fig. 2 - Une girouette.

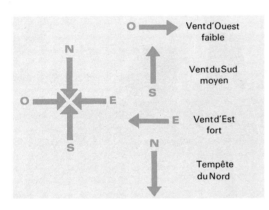

Fig. 3 - Comment on indique la direction et la force des vents.

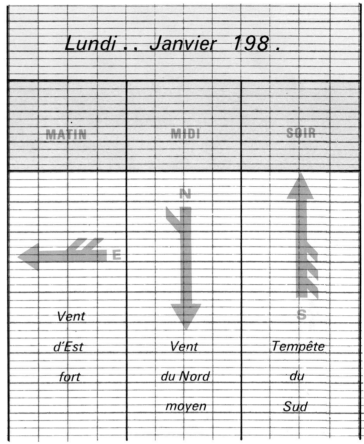

Fig. 4 - Faisons un tableau des vents.

En **hivernage,** le vent souffle de la mer. Il pousse de gros nuages et nous apporte de la pluie.

Sur la grande mer, sur le fleuve, sur la lagune, le pêcheur connaît bien le vent. C'est le vent qui souffle dans sa voile et qui fait avancer sa pirogue. Il est bien utile lorsqu'il est modéré. Mais, quand il souffle en tempête, il fait chavirer les petits bateaux.

Lorsqu'il fait grand vent, le linge de la ménagère sèche plus vite.

Dans certains villages d'Afrique, on a construit des moulins actionnés par le vent. On les appelle des éoliennes. Elles tournent sous l'action du vent, font monter l'eau des puits et produisent du courant électrique.

QUESTIONS ET EXERCICES

Faisons un tableau des vents (voir figure 4). Il nous faut, pour cela, connaître la direction du vent. Pour connaître cette direction fabriquons une girouette. La girouette tourne sur un axe. Les points cardinaux sont fixes. L'hélice de la girouette nous montre d'où souffle le vent (voir figure 2).

De quelle direction souffle, en général, le vent · en saison sèche? De quelle direction souffle-t-il en hivernage?

RÉSUMÉ

Le vent, c'est de l'air qui se déplace. Sur la mer, le vent fait avancer la pirogue du pêcheur. En saison sèche, le vent est brûlant : c'est l'harmattan. Le vent d'hivernage souffle de la mer. Il pousse de gros nuages. Il nous apporte la pluie.

Fig. 1 - Qu'il fait froid ce matin !

Photo Hoa-Qui.

Fig. 2 - A midi, on recherche l'ombre.

OBSERVONS

Autour de nous : Le matin, il fait froid. Que font les enfants qui viennent à l'école ? Comment sont-ils habillés à midi ? le soir ?

Le thermomètre : Montrons les diverses parties du thermomètre de la classe. Soufflons dessus ou mettons-le un petit instant au soleil. Que voyons-nous ?

Les documents : Sur la *figure 1*, c'est le matin. Il fait froid. Sur la *figure 2*, il est midi. Il fait chaud. A quoi le voyons-nous ?

LEÇON

C'est le **matin.** Le soleil n'est pas encore levé. Mamadou part pour l'école. Il se pelotonne dans son boubou. Il tremble. Il a froid.

A **midi,** le soleil est au-dessus de nos têtes. Il fait très chaud. Mamadou dort à l'ombre. Pour les hommes, c'est l'heure de la sieste.

Le **soir,** quand le soleil descend puis se couche, le froid retombe sur la terre. Dans toutes les maisons, on allume du feu.

Dans notre classe, nous avons un **thermomètre.** Ce thermomètre se compose d'un réservoir et d'un tube en verre. Le réservoir et le tube contiennent un liquide.

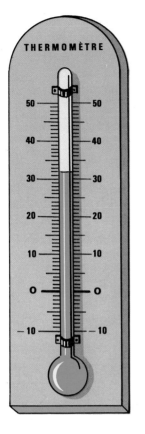

Fig. 3 - Un thermomètre.

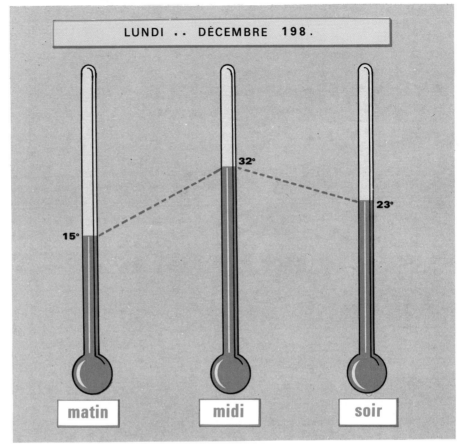

LUNDI .. DÉCEMBRE 198.

32°

15°

23°

matin   midi   soir

Fig. 4 - Le tableau des températures.

Dans certains thermomètres, ce liquide est argenté : c'est du **mercure.** Dans d'autres il est rouge ou bleu : c'est de l'**alcool.**

Des 2 côtés du tube, nous lisons des chiffres *(voir figure 3)*. Quand il fait chaud, le liquide monte dans le tube en verre. Quand il fait froid, il redescend.

Ce matin, le thermomètre indiquait **15 degrés.** A midi, il marquait **32 degrés.**

Le maître a dit que la **température** de la classe était de 32 degrés.

Au mois de janvier, nous avons eu froid. Le thermomètre est descendu à 12 degrés. Mais, au mois d'avril, il a fait très chaud. Nous avons relevé, dans notre classe, une température de 35 degrés.

QUESTIONS ET EXERCICES

Notons, le matin, à midi et le soir, les températures dans notre classe. Faisons un tableau des températures comme celui de la figure 4.

Quel est, dans notre pays, le mois le plus froid ? le mois le plus chaud ?

Quelle est la plus basse température relevée dans notre classe ? Quelle est la plus forte ?

Quand ont-elles été relevées ?

RÉSUMÉ

Le thermomètre sert à mesurer la température. Le thermomètre « descend » quand il fait froid. Il « monte » quand il fait chaud. La température varie au cours de la journée. Elle est basse le matin et le soir. Elle est haute à midi. La température varie aussi avec les mois de l'année.

13 LE TEMPS QU'IL FAIT : LES NUAGES ET LA PLUIE

Photo Vincent/AAA-Photo.

Fig. 1 - Le ciel se couvre de gros nuages : il va pleuvoir.

Brume

Grand soleil

Ciel un peu nuageux

Ciel nuageux

Pluie

Fig. 2 - Comment on indique l'état du ciel.

OBSERVONS

Autour de nous : Faisons bouillir de l'eau dans une casserole. Quand l'eau bout, une sorte de fumée monte. Au contact d'une assiette froide, que se forme-t-il ?

Que voit-on le matin, de bonne heure, qui semble flotter au-dessus du marigot ?

Les documents : Que voyons-nous, dans le ciel, sur la *figure 1* ? En quelle saison sommes-nous ? Va-t-il faire beau ? Va-t-il pleuvoir ?

LEÇON

Nous voyons que, peu de temps après la pluie, les flaques d'eau de la cour sont séchées par le soleil. Cette eau s'est transformée en **vapeur** qui monte et flotte dans l'air. On ne la voit pas.

Le matin, surtout en saison sèche, nous voyons une sorte de fumée blanche au-dessus du marigot. C'est de la **vapeur d'eau.** Elle mouille les herbes. On l'appelle de la **brume** ou du **brouillard.**

Dans le ciel, le vent pousse les **nuages.** Il y en a de petits, blancs comme du coton. Il y a aussi de gros nuages noirs. Comme la vapeur

30

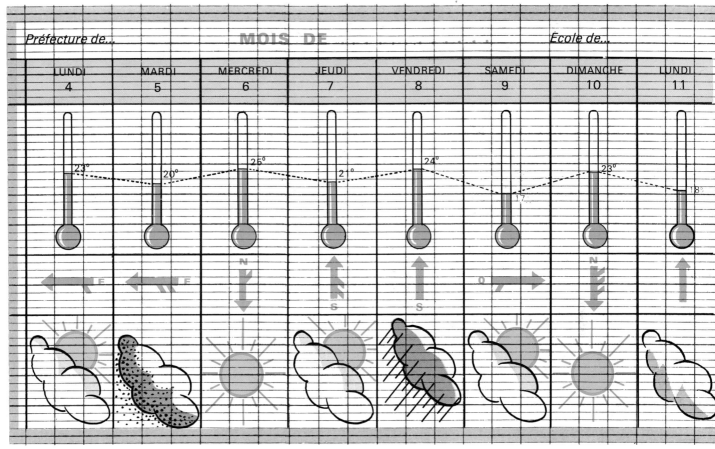

Fig. 3 - Apprenons à faire un tableau du temps.

d'eau qui frappe l'assiette forme des gouttes, les gouttes de vapeur d'eau s'assemblent pour former les nuages. Lorsqu'il fait plus froid, que le vent faiblit, ces petites gouttes se réunissent les unes aux autres. Quand elles sont trop lourdes pour flotter dans l'air, elles tombent. **Il pleut.**

En **hivernage,** le ciel est toujours couvert de nuages. Le soleil ne se montre que rarement. La pluie tombe souvent en grosses gouttes sous forme de **tornades.**

La pluie vous trempe en un clin d'œil. Pour sortir, les maîtres portent des bottes, des imperméables ou un parapluie. Le paysan se protège sous un large chapeau ou sous une feuille de bananier.

QUESTIONS ET EXERCICES

Établissez chaque semaine un tableau des pluies comme vous en avez fait un pour les températures. Vous y ajouterez la date de la première pluie, le nombre de jours de pluie.

Dresser, chaque mois, un tableau du temps comme celui de la figure 3. Porter les températures, les vents, la pluie et les nuages.

RÉSUMÉ

La brume est une fumée blanche qui flotte, le matin, au-dessus du marigot. Les nuages, formés de fines gouttelettes d'eau, sont poussés par le vent.

Lorsqu'il fait froid, ces gouttelettes grossissent et tombent sous forme de pluie.

14 LA SAISON SÈCHE

Photo Hoa-Qui.

Fig. 1 - En saison sèche, il y a peu d'eau : les rochers du bord du Congo
sont découverts. Comparer avec la figure 1, page 34.

OBSERVONS

Autour de nous : la nature. Quelle est la couleur de la campagne ? Comment sont les arbres ? Y a-t-il beaucoup d'eau à la source, dans le marigot ?

Les animaux : Ont-ils beaucoup de nourriture ? Où la trouvent-ils ? Sont-ils gros et gras ?

Les hommes : A quels travaux se livrent-ils dans les champs ?

Les documents : Sur la *figure 1*, nous voyons un fleuve d'Afrique. Cette rivière a-t-elle beaucoup d'eau ? Pourquoi ?

La *figure 2* nous montre des paysans au travail. Que font-ils ? En quelle saison sommes-nous ?

LEÇON

Depuis le mois d'octobre, il n'a pas plu une seule fois. Le vent d'est, l'**harmattan,** souffle depuis des semaines. Partout les herbes sèchent. La campagne jaunit. Il n'y a presque plus d'eau à la source. Le marigot n'est plus qu'un mince filet d'eau qui, bientôt, tarira. Il fait très chaud. Les **récoltes** mûrissent.

Les cultivateurs **moissonnent,** puis battent leurs céréales. Ils ramassent précieusement le grain dans les greniers. Ils réparent maisons et clôtures avec les lianes de la forêt et la longue paille de la brousse. Puis ils se reposent en attendant les premières pluies.

Fig. 2 - En saison sèche, les récoltes sont mûres
et les paysans moissonnent.

Beaucoup de villageois profitent du beau temps pour faire de longs **voyages.** Les routes et les ponts ont été réparés et les fleuves, presque taris, sont faciles à franchir.

Les vaches et les moutons cherchent au bord du marigot une maigre nourriture. Ils s'écartent du village, n'y rentrent pas toujours le soir et deviennent la proie des panthères et des autres bêtes sauvages. Les vaches ne donnent plus de lait. Les animaux sont tellement maigres qu'ils n'ont plus que les os et la peau.

La **saison sèche** est aussi la saison des **feux de brousse** qui s'allument tous les soirs autour des villages. Aidés par la sécheresse, poussés par le vent, ils dévastent chaque année d'immenses étendues.

QUESTIONS ET EXERCICES

A quelle époque commence la saison sèche dans notre région ? A quelle date se termine-t-elle ? Combien de mois dure-t-elle ? Les sources de notre village tarissent-elles en saison sèche ? A partir de quel mois ? Le marigot est-il quelquefois à sec ? Quand ?

Avez-vous vu des feux de brousse près de votre village ? Quand ont-ils éclaté ? Décrivez-les ?

RÉSUMÉ

La saison sèche commence en septembre ou octobre et se termine en mai ou en juin. Il n'y a plus d'eau à la source ni au marigot. Tout se dessèche.
Les hommes et les bêtes souffrent. C'est le moment de la récolte, des grands voyages et aussi des feux de brousse.

15 LA SAISON DES PLUIES

Photo Hoa-Qui.

Fig. 1 - Il a plu, le Congo s'est gonflé d'eau et recouvre une partie des rochers du bord.

OBSERVONS

Autour de nous : Les pluies ont commencé. Quelle est la couleur de la campagne ? Y a-t-il beaucoup d'eau dans le marigot ? **Les animaux** trouvent-ils à nouveau de la nourriture ? A quels **travaux** se livrent les hommes du village ?

Les documents : Sur la *figure 1*, nous voyons la même rivière que celle de la *p. 32.* A-t-elle beaucoup d'eau ?
Sur la *figure 2*, les paysans sont aux champs. Que font-ils ?

LEÇON

Dans notre région, le temps change au mois de .... Le ciel qui était toujours bleu commence à se couvrir de nuages. Il pleut, d'abord de temps en temps, puis, bientôt, tous les jours. Souvent le tonnerre gronde. Les **tornades** font rage. L'**hivernage** ou **saison des pluies** est commencé. Dans certaines régions, il va maintenant pleuvoir nuit et jour.

Le marigot qui était à sec se gonfle. Ses eaux boueuses montent rapidement. Elles débordent, inondent les rives et les fertilisent.

Quel remue-ménage dans les champs ! Avec leurs dabas, leurs charrues, hommes, femmes et enfants labourent la terre.

34

Fig. 2 - Après avoir labouré le sol, on écrase les mottes de terre pour préparer les nouvelles semailles.

C'est la **saison des labours** et des **semailles.** Tout ce que l'on sème sort rapidement de terre. Partout, l'herbe pousse. Toute la campagne reverdit. Les animaux trouvent de quoi manger. Ils redeviennent gros et gras.

Mais la pluie continue. Il fait froid.

Beaucoup de ponts sont emportés par les rivières qui coulent avec violence. En période de crue, les routes sont ravinées par les eaux qui ruissellent ; certaines deviennent inutilisables. Les camions circulent difficilement. Le courrier a toujours du retard. Il ne fait pas bon voyager en hivernage.

Lorsqu'il pleut, que le vent souffle, qu'il fait froid, il fait si bon près du feu !

QUESTIONS ET EXERCICES

A quelle époque commence l'hivernage dans notre région ? A quelle date finit-il ? Combien de mois dure-t-il ? Quel est le mois où il pleut le plus ?

Connaissons-nous d'autres régions où l'hivernage est plus long ou plus court que chez nous ?

Connaissons-nous des régions qui ont deux saisons des pluies ?

Fait-il chaud en hivernage ? Y a-t-il des moments où il fait plus froid ? Quand ? Notre marigot déborde-t-il ?

●

RÉSUMÉ

L'hivernage commence, suivant les régions, en juin ou juillet et se termine en octobre ou novembre. Il pleut sans cesse. Les marigots débordent. La nature reverdit. C'est la saison des labours et des semailles.

16 L'EAU DANS LA NATURE

Fig. 1 - Expérience du sable et de l'argile.

Fig. 2 - Un puits et une source.

OBSERVONS

Autour de nous : La source et le marigot de mon village.

Les documents : La *figure 1* nous montre l'expérience que nous allons faire avec notre maître à l'aide d'une boîte, de sable et d'argile et dans laquelle nous allons verser de l'eau.

La *figure 3* est la carte du marigot de mon village. Montrons sa source, un pont, un jardin, les 2 rives, l'endroit où le marigot se jette dans la rivière.

LEÇON

L'eau que nous versons dans notre boîte **s'infiltre** dans le **sable**. Elle est arrêtée par l'**argile**. Creusons un trou avec notre doigt dans le sable : l'eau y apparaît. Perçons le côté de notre boîte : l'eau sort.

De la même façon, l'eau de pluie s'infiltre dans les **sols sableux.** Les **sols argileux** l'arrêtent et elle forme, dans le sol, des **nappes d'eau.** En creusant un **puits,** nous atteignons cette nappe d'eau. Mais, sous terre, cette eau se creuse un passage. Elle sort au flanc de la colline et forme une **source** *(figure 2)*. Les femmes du village viennent y puiser de l'eau.

LA SOURCE. LE MARIGOT

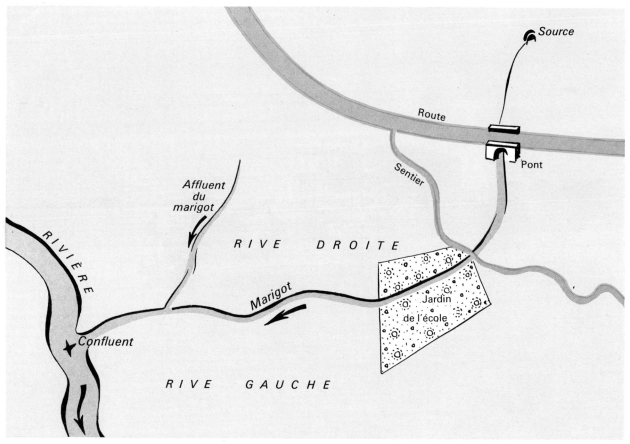

Fig. 3 - Le marigot de mon village.

Mais cette eau coule et se creuse un petit chemin. D'autres petits filets d'eau se sont joints au premier pour former le **ruisseau** ou le **marigot** de mon village.

Le marigot coule dans une petite **vallée**. Sur ses **rives,** les villageois ont installé leurs jardins qui sont ainsi faciles à arroser. Le marigot n'est pas encore bien large. Nous le traversons facilement à gué ou sur un tronc d'arbre. Le marigot se jette dans la grande **rivière** qui emporte ses eaux vers la mer. L'endroit où il rejoint la grande rivière est un **confluent.** Le marigot est un **affluent** de la grande rivière.

Notre petit marigot est très utile. Il permet à plusieurs villages de vivre car il leur fournit l'eau indispensable.

QUESTIONS ET EXERCICES

Y a-t-il une ou plusieurs sources autour de notre village? Où coulent-elles? Ont-elles de l'eau toute l'année? Plaçons-les sur le plan du village.

En nous aidant de la figure 3, faisons le plan du marigot du village. Marquons sa source, son cours, le sens du courant, la rive droite et la rive gauche. S'il a des affluents, traçons-les. A quels villages, notre marigot fournit-il de l'eau?

RÉSUMÉ

L'eau s'infiltre dans le sable. Elle est arrêtée par l'argile. Au bas de la colline, elle sort de terre et forme une source.
Le marigot coule dans une petite vallée. Sur ses rives, il y a de nombreux jardins. Il se jette dans la grande rivière. C'est un affluent de la rivière.

17 RIVIÈRES ET FLEUVES

Fig. 1 - Pour traverser le Sénégal, lorsqu'il n'y a pas de pont, on utilise un bac.

OBSERVONS

Autour de nous : Y a-t-il un **fleuve** dans notre région? Comment l'appelle-t-on? Est-il large et profond?
Y a-t-il, près de notre village, des étendues d'eau qui ne coulent pas? Comment les appelle-t-on?

Les documents : La *figure 1* représente un grand fleuve. Est-il large? Comment le traverse-t-on? La *figure 2* représente un lac. Que voyons-nous sur ses bords? Que viennent y faire les animaux?

LEÇON

Le **marigot** s'est jeté dans la **rivière**. Plusieurs rivières se sont réunies les unes aux autres pour former un **fleuve**.

Le **fleuve** est très large. On le traverse sur un grand **pont** ou sur un **bac.** Il est long de plusieurs centaines de kilomètres. Sur sa **rive droite** et sur sa **rive gauche,** il reçoit de nombreux **affluents**.

Il arrose de grandes plaines et de nombreuses villes. Parfois, le fleuve tombe brusquement d'une grande hauteur. Il forme une **chute**.

Le fleuve est profond. Il porte des pirogues et des bateaux à fond plat qu'on appelle des chalands.

Photo Picou/AAA-Photo.

Fig. 2 - Dans la savane, un troupeau de zèbres vient boire au bord du lac.

Devant les chutes, les bateaux doivent s'arrêter et il faut transborder les marchandises. En hivernage, le fleuve déborde. Il inonde ses rives et fertilise d'immenses rizières. Dans ses eaux, les villageois pêchent de nombreux poissons.

Après avoir traversé et arrosé plusieurs pays, le fleuve se jette dans la mer par une large **embouchure.** Quelquefois, à l'intérieur des terres, nous nous trouvons au bord d'une étendue d'eau douce et qui ne coule pas. On dirait qu'elle dort. Elle forme une **mare.** Une grande mare est un **étang.** Un grand étang est un **lac.**

Dans la mare, l'eau monte en saison des pluies. Elle baisse en saison sèche. Sur les bords de la mare, à mesure que l'eau baisse, les habitants du village cultivent des légumes. Les animaux viennent y boire.

QUESTIONS ET EXERCICES

Comment s'appelle le fleuve de notre région? Où prend-il sa source? Quels pays traverse-t-il? Où se jette-t-il? Comment le traverse-t-on dans notre village?

Le fleuve de notre région porte-t-il des bateaux? Quelles ressources apporte-t-il aux habitants de notre village? La pêche y est-elle bonne?

Y a-t-il, près de notre village, une mare, un étang ou un lac? Comment l'appellent les villageois? Que fait-on sur ses bords?

RÉSUMÉ

Les petites rivières se réunissent pour former un fleuve. Long, large, profond, le fleuve fertilise ses rives, porte des bateaux et fournit du poisson. Une petite étendue d'eau douce est une mare ou un étang. Un grand étang s'appelle un lac.

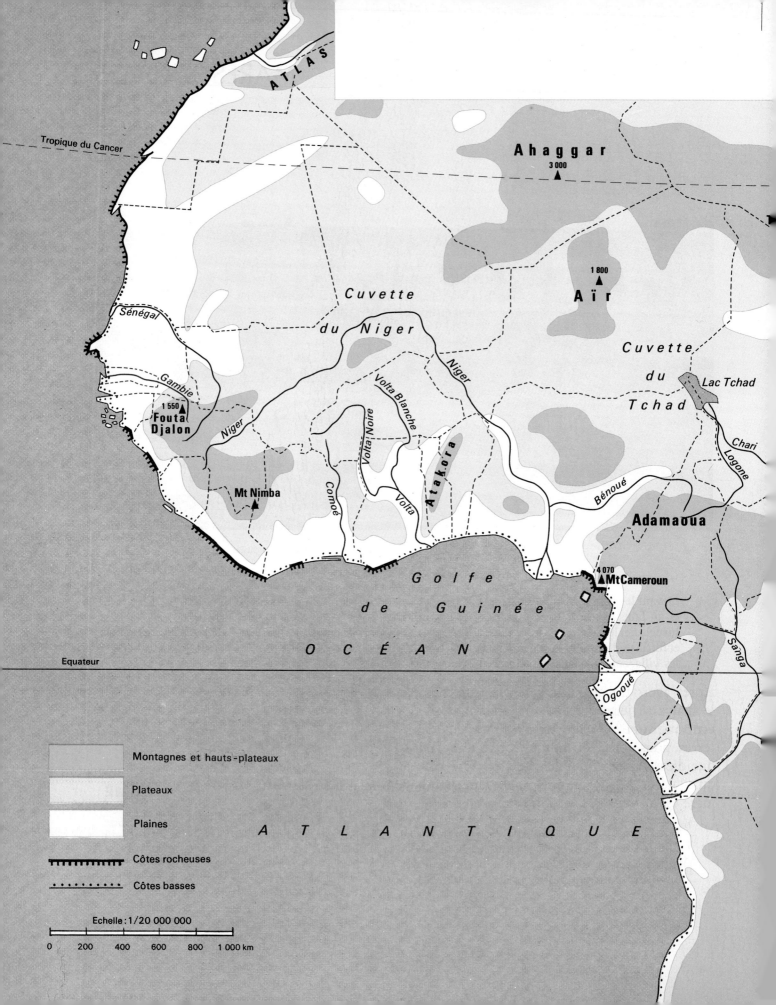

ATLAS

Tropique du Cancer

Ahaggar
3 000 ▲

1 800
▲
Aïr

Cuvette
du Niger

Cuvette
du
Tchad

Sénégal

Gambie

Niger

Volta Blanche

Niger

Lac Tchad

Chari

Logone

1 550 ▲
Fouta
Djalon

Niger

Volta Noire

Atakora

Bénoué

Adamaoua

▲ Mt Nimba

Comoé

Volta

4 070
▲ Mt Cameroun

Golfe
de   Guinée

Sanga

OCÉAN

Equateur

Ogooué

Montagnes et hauts-plateaux

Plateaux

Plaines

A T L A N T I Q U E

Côtes rocheuses

Côtes basses

Echelle : 1/20 000 000

0   200   400   600   800   1 000 km

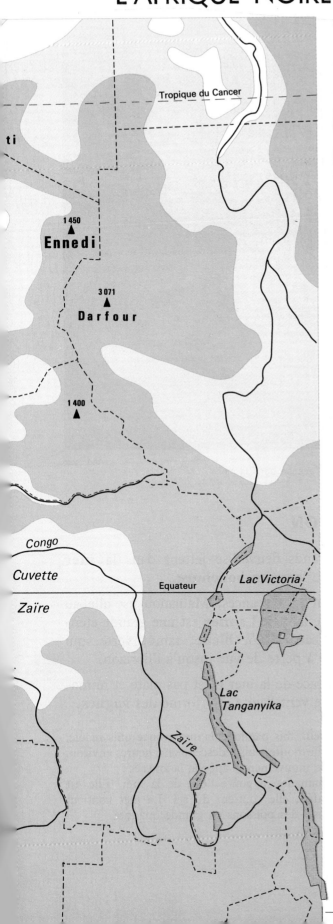

OBSERVONS

La carte nous montre le relief, les côtes et les fleuves de l'Afrique Noire.

Nous y voyons, en bistre foncé, les régions montagneuses.

Voyez, par exemple, le Fouta Djalon, le mont Cameroun et l'Adamaoua.

Les plateaux apparaissent dans un bistre plus clair.

L'Afrique Noire est un pays de plateaux.

En blanc, enfin, nous trouvons les plaines, situées surtout au bord de la mer,

Les côtes de l'Afrique Noire bordent l'océan Atlantique.

Les côtes rocheuses sont indiquées par des traits épais ; les côtes basses et sablonneuses sont bordées de points.

Les grands fleuves de l'Afrique Noire sont portés sur la carte :

Montrez le Sénégal, le Niger, la Volta, le Congo, qui se jettent dans l'océan Atlantique ; le Logone et le Chari se jettent dans le lac Tchad.

QUESTIONS ET EXERCICES

Montrons, sur la carte, une région de montagnes, de plateaux, de plaine.

Suivons du doigt la côte de l'Afrique Noire.

Où est-elle rocheuse ? où est-elle basse et sablonneuse ?

Suivons les fleuves depuis leur source jusqu'à leur embouchure.

Où se jettent le Niger, le Chari ? Montrons les affluents du Congo. Comment s'appellent-ils ?

19 LA MER

Fig. 1 - En avant de Dakar, la presqu'île s'avance dans la mer.

AAA-Photo.

OBSERVONS

Autour de nous : Si nous habitons au bord de la mer, notons sa couleur? Relevons, pendant plusieurs jours, l'heure où la mer est basse ; l'heure où elle est haute.

Les documents : La *figure 1* nous montre une grande pointe de terre qui s'avance dans la mer. Montrons du doigt les endroits où la mer pénètre dans les terres.
La *figure 2* nous montre de grands rochers entourés par la mer de toutes parts.

LEÇON

Les grands fleuves se jettent dans la **mer** par une large **embouchure.**

Pendant les vacances, Mamadou est allé au bord de la mer. La **mer** est une grande étendue d'eau, tantôt **bleue**, tantôt verte, qui s'étend à perte de vue jusqu'à l'horizon.

La surface de la mer n'est pas plate et immobile. Le vent l'agite et y forme des **vagues.**

Deux fois par jour, la mer avance puis recule. Elle monte, puis redescend en 6 heures environ. Ce mouvement s'appelle la **marée.**
Mamadou a goûté l'eau de la mer. Elle est **salée,** elle contient du sel. La mer contient aussi des poissons en grande quantité.

Fig. 2 - Entourée d'eau de toutes parts, l'île de Gorée est reliée à Dakar par un service de bateaux.

Le bord de la mer s'appelle la **côte.** Aux environs de Dakar, comme nous le montre la *figure 1*, la côte est très **découpée.** De petites pointes de terre s'avancent dans la mer : on les appelle des **caps.** En d'autres endroits, la mer s'enfonce dans la terre et forme des **baies.** Une grande baie s'appelle un **golfe.**

Parfois de petites étendues de terre sont entièrement entourées par la mer comme sur la *figure 2*. On les appelle des **îles.** Si une étendue de terre est entourée par la mer sauf en un seul endroit, c'est presque une île : on la nomme **presqu'île.** La *gravure 1* nous montre une grande presqu'île. **Dakar** est construit sur la **presqu'île du Cap-Vert.**

QUESTIONS ET EXERCICES

Cherchons des gravures qui nous montrent la mer et les côtes en Afrique.

Montrons, sur ces gravures, un cap, une pointe, une baie, un golfe, une presqu'île, une île.

Si nous habitons au bord de la mer, faisons évaporer un litre d'eau de mer. Que reste-t-il dans notre assiette ? Pesons le sel qui y reste.

RÉSUMÉ

La mer est une immense étendue d'eau salée. La mer monte et descend deux fois par jour : c'est la marée.
Un cap est une pointe de terre qui s'avance dans la mer. La mer qui s'enfonce dans les terres forme un golfe. Une île est entourée par la mer de tous côtés; une presqu'île est entourée d'eau sur trois côtés.

20 LES CÔTES

Photo Vincent/AAA-Photo.

Fig. 1 - Sur la côte rocheuse, les vagues ont découpé des pointes et des creux.

OBSERVONS

Autour de nous : Si nous habitons au bord de la mer, promenons-nous sur la côte. Est-elle bordée de sable ou de rochers ? Est-elle basse ou haute ? droite ou découpée ?

Les documents : La *figure 1* nous montre une côte bordée de grands rochers. Est-elle haute ou basse ? droite ou découpée ?

La côte de la *figure 2* est-elle encore bordée de rochers ? Est-elle haute ? Est-elle découpée ?

LEÇON

Nous avons vu, dans la leçon précédente, que le bord de la mer s'appelle la **côte**. Les *figures* nous montrent que toutes les côtes d'Afrique ne se ressemblent pas.

La côte que nous voyons sur la *figure 1* est bordée d'énormes rochers. C'est pourquoi on l'appelle une **côte rocheuse**. Elle s'élève à pic au-dessus de la mer. Elle est très **haute** et aussi très **découpée**. Une côte rocheuse présente de nombreux caps, des golfes, des baies et des presqu'îles.

Souvent, tout près de la côte, on voit des îles, nombreuses aussi. Une côte rocheuse est très difficile à aborder. La nuit, la lumière des phares facilite l'approche de la côte.

LES CÔTES 20

Photo Serv. Information de la Côte-d'Ivoire.

Fig. 2 - Une plage sablonneuse ombragée de cocotiers sur le rivage de la Côte-d'Ivoire.

Sur une côte rocheuse, dans les baies, on peut trouver de bons **abris** pour les pirogues et les bateaux. On peut aussi, facilement, y établir un **port** pour les grands bateaux.

La *figure 2* représente une côte tout à fait différente de la précédente. Elle n'est plus bordée de rochers, mais de sable. On l'appelle, pour cette raison, une **côte sablonneuse.**
Elle est **basse** et descend tout doucement vers la mer. Elle est presque droite.

On y trouve peu d'abris pour les bateaux.

Elle est parfois bordée de petits lacs qu'on appelle des **lagunes.** Elle a des **plages** de sable fin où les habitants viennent se baigner et se reposer.

QUESTIONS ET EXERCICES

Cherchons des gravures représentant des côtes africaines : côtes rocheuses, côtes sablonneuses, une plage, un phare.
Si vous habitez au bord de la mer, décrivez la côte de votre région.

Avec de la terre glaise et des pierres, modelons une côte rocheuse avec des caps, des golfes, une presqu'île, des îles.
Modelons, à côté, une côte basse, bordée de sable.

RÉSUMÉ

Le bord de la mer s'appelle la côte. Une côte rocheuse est haute et découpée. Elle a de nombreux abris, mais ses rochers la rendent dangereuse pour les bateaux.
Une côte sablonneuse est basse et rectiligne. Elle a des plages, mais pas d'abris.

45

21 LES ZONES DE CLIMAT ET DE VÉGÉTATION

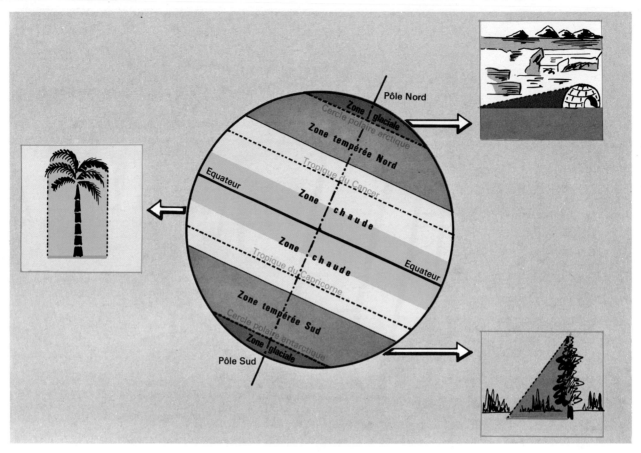

Fig. 1 - Les zones de climat et de végétation.

OBSERVONS

Autour de nous : Plaçons une lampe allumée à côté du globe terrestre et à hauteur de l'Équateur. Mesurons avec une ficelle la distance de la lampe à l'Équateur et aux pôles. Quelle est la distance la plus courte ?

Les documents : Ils représentent des régions différentes de la terre au même moment de l'année. Sur la *figure 2*, la neige et la glace recouvrent le sol. La *figure 3* est un coin de forêt en Afrique Noire. Y fait-il froid ? Pourquoi ? Le voyons-nous ?

LEÇON

Si nous plaçons une lampe à côté du **globe terrestre**, à hauteur de l'**Équateur**, nous constatons, en mesurant avec une ficelle, que toutes les régions proches de l'Équateur sont plus près de la lampe que les deux Pôles.

Cette partie du globe est chaude alors que les Pôles ne le sont pas. Ce que nous constatons ainsi se produit presque de la même façon pour la terre et le soleil. Les rayons du soleil frappent la terre à peu près **d'aplomb**, à l'**Équateur.** Il y fait très chaud. Au contraire, ils arrivent à peine à lécher les Pôles. C'est pourquoi il y fait très froid.

La région de la terre située des deux côtés de

Photo R. Bonnardel-Rapho.

Fig. 2 - Dans la zone froide.

Photo Vincent/AAA-Photo.

Fig. 3 - Dans la zone chaude.

l'Équateur et que l'on appelle la zone équatoriale ou **zone chaude**.

L'Afrique Noire tout entière se trouve dans la zone chaude.

Les régions situées autour des Pôles sont très froides. Entièrement couvertes de neige et de glace, on les appelle des **zones glaciales.**

Il y a, sur la terre, deux zones glaciales, l'une au **Pôle Nord**, l'autre au **Pôle Sud**.

Entre la zone chaude et les deux zones glaciales se trouvent deux zones où il ne fait ni trop chaud ni trop froid. Ce sont les **zones tempérées.**

Les zones tempérées sont les régions les plus riches du globe. La France se trouve dans la zone tempérée Nord.

QUESTIONS ET EXERCICES

Traçons, sur le globe terrestre, la zone chaude, les zones froides et les zones tempérées. Dans quelle zone se trouve notre pays?

Dessinons un globe. Plaçons-y l'Équateur et les Pôles. Traçons, puis colorions, comme sur la figure 1, la zone chaude, les zones glaciales et les zones tempérées.

RÉSUMÉ

La terre a une zone chaude des deux côtés de l'Équateur et deux zones glaciales, au Pôle Nord et au Pôle Sud. Entre la zone chaude et les deux zones glaciales se trouvent deux zones tempérées où il ne fait ni trop chaud ni trop froid.

22 PAYSAGES D'AFRIQUE : LA FORÊT

Fig. 1 - Une forêt très épaisse en République Centrafricaine traversée par une rivière, la Bouali, qui tombe en cascade.

OBSERVONS

Autour de nous (si nous habitons la forêt) : Y pleut-il beaucoup? Combien y a-t-il de saisons des pluies? Quels sont les mois où il pleut le plus? Y a-t-il des mois où il ne pleut pas du tout?

Les documents : Que représentent-ils? Y voyons-nous beaucoup d'arbres? Sommes-nous dans un pays sec ou dans un pays humide? A quoi le voyons-nous? Le paysage de notre région ressemble-t-il à ceux des documents?

LEÇON

Tous les pays d'Afrique ne se ressemblent pas. Il y a des pays où il pleut beaucoup et des régions où il ne pleut presque pas.

Dans les pays situés des deux côtés de l'Équateur, il fait très chaud, très humide et il pleut très souvent. Il y a, dans ces pays, **deux saisons des pluies.**

Ces régions sont couvertes de **forêts.** La **forêt** est très épaisse. On y circule difficilement. Les arbres, très serrés, sont si hauts qu'on en voit à peine la cime. Ils forment une grande voûte qui empêche le soleil et la lumière de passer. Ces arbres restent toujours verts *(figure I)*.

48

Fig. 2 - Dans la forêt, une clairière avec des habitations et des cultures.

Fig. 3 - La récolte du palmiste en Côte-d'Ivoire.

Dans cette forêt, on abat de grands arbres comme l'acajou ou l'okoumé, qui sont des **bois précieux.**

Dans les clairières, les habitants ont construit leur village *(figure 2)*. Ils y cultivent l'igname, le manioc, la patate et les bananiers. Le riz a beaucoup de mal à mûrir.

Les habitants de la forêt grimpent aux palmiers pour y récolter les **palmistes** *(figure 3)*. Les **plantations** commencent à produire beaucoup de **cacao**, de **café** et de **caoutchouc.**

L'homme élève très peu de bétail car, comme les arbres sont très serrés, il n'y a pas de pâturages et il y a encore beaucoup de mouches tsé-tsé dans la forêt.

QUESTIONS ET EXERCICES

Habitons-nous en forêt? Qui de nous y est allé? Où? Y pleut-il beaucoup? A quelle époque?
Quels sont les principaux arbres de la forêt? Quelle est leur hauteur? Abat-on beaucoup d'arbres en forêt? Qu'en fait-on?

Que cultive-t-on dans les clairières?
Faisons la carte de l'Afrique Noire (voir pp. 52-53).
Sur notre dessin, colorions en vert les pays de forêt.

RÉSUMÉ

Dans certaines régions d'Afrique, des deux côtés de l'Équateur, il pleut très souvent. Le sol est couvert d'une immense forêt. Les hommes vivent dans les clairières et ont beaucoup de mal à cultiver le sol. Ils abattent les grands arbres qui donnent du bois précieux.

23 LA SAVANE. LE DÉSERT

Fig. 1 - Dans la savane, de hautes herbes et quelques arbres.

OBSERVONS

Autour de nous : Si notre pays est un pays de savane (ou de désert), notons la durée de la saison des pluies. Quelles plantes poussent dans notre région ? Quels animaux y élève-t-on ?

Les documents : Voyez-vous encore un pays de forêt sur la *fig. 1* ? Y a-t-il de grands arbres ? Comment les nomme-t-on ? Trouve-t-on beaucoup d'arbres sur la *figure 2* ? Comment sont-ils groupés et comment les nomme-t-on ?

LEÇON

Nous quittons la forêt et nous remontons vers le **Nord.** Nous arrivons dans des pays qui n'ont plus qu'**une seule saison des pluies :** saison de plus en plus courte, à mesure que nous avançons vers le Nord.

La forêt a presque disparu. Parmi les hautes herbes et les buissons d'épineux, on voit encore quelques arbres : des karités, des nérés, des baobabs. C'est la **savane.**

La savane est la **région de cultures** de l'Afrique Noire. Les paysans y cultivent le riz, le mil, le fonio, les arachides et le coton. Ils élèves de nombreux **troupeaux.**

La savane, qui a du gros gibier, est aussi une région de **grande chasse.**

50

Photo S.-D. Lajoux.

Fig. 2 - Dans le désert du Sahara, les habitations se groupent près des oasis.

Continuons encore notre voyage vers le Nord. Il fait de plus en plus chaud le jour, mais de plus en plus froid la nuit. Il ne pleut presque plus.

Il n'y a plus d'arbres; seulement quelques buissons d'épineux et, parfois, un peu d'herbe. On ne voit que du sable et des pierres à perte de vue. C'est le **désert.**

Les habitants du désert ne construisent pas de maisons. Ils vivent sous des **tentes** qu'ils déplacent pour suivre leurs troupeaux. Ce sont des **nomades.**

Ils élèvent des **chameaux** qui peuvent rester plusieurs jours sans boire. On rencontre de temps à autre un point d'eau avec des palmiers. C'est une **oasis** *(figure 2).* Le grand désert du **Sahara** borde tout le Nord de l'Afrique Noire.

QUESTIONS ET EXERCICES

Combien y a-t-il de saisons de pluies dans la savane?
Quelles plantes y cultive-t-on? Quels animaux y élève-t-on?

Pleut-il beaucoup dans le désert?
Quel animal y élève-t-on? Pourquoi? Comment appelle-t-on un point d'eau?
Continuons notre carte de l'Afrique Noire (voir pp. 52-53). Colorions en marron les pays de savane et en jaune le désert.

RÉSUMÉ

Dans la savane, il n'y a qu'une saison des pluies. La savane est la région des hautes herbes, des cultures variées, de l'élevage et de la grande chasse. Dans le désert, il ne pleut plus. Il n'y pousse rien. L'animal du désert est le chameau.

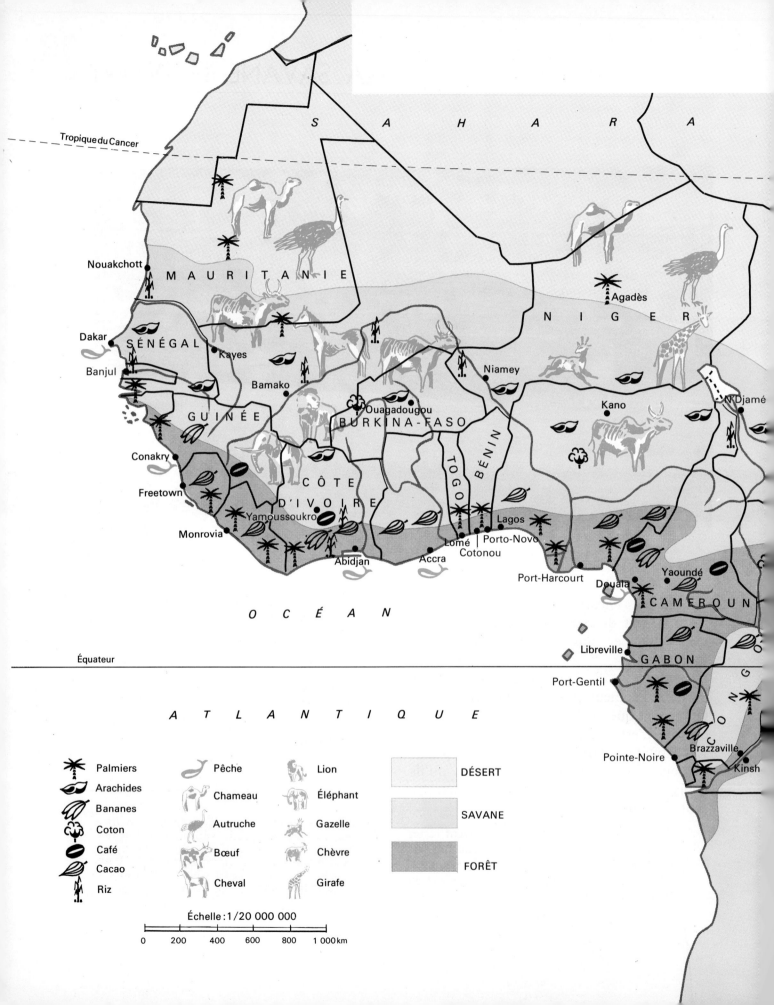

S A H A R A

Tropique du Cancer

MAURITANIE

Nouakchott

Dakar
SÉNÉGAL
Kayes
Banjul
Bamako

N I G E R

Agadès

Niamey

Kano

NDjamé

GUINÉE

Conakry

Freetown

Monrovia

Yamoussoukro

BURKINA-FASO

Ouagadougou

CÔTE
D'IVOIRE

Abidjan

Accra

T
O
G
O

B
É
N
I
N

Lomé
Cotonou

Porto-Novo

Lagos

Port-Harcourt

Douala

Yaoundé

CAMEROUN

O C É A N

Équateur

Libreville

GABON

Port-Gentil

C
O
N
G
O

A T L A N T I Q U E

Pointe-Noire

Brazzaville

Kinsh

Légende

Palmiers	Pêche	Lion	
Arachides	Chameau	Éléphant	
Bananes	Autruche	Gazelle	
Coton	Bœuf	Chèvre	
Café	Cheval	Girafe	
Cacao			
Riz			

DÉSERT

SAVANE

FORÊT

Échelle : 1/20 000 000

0   200   400   600   800   1 000 km

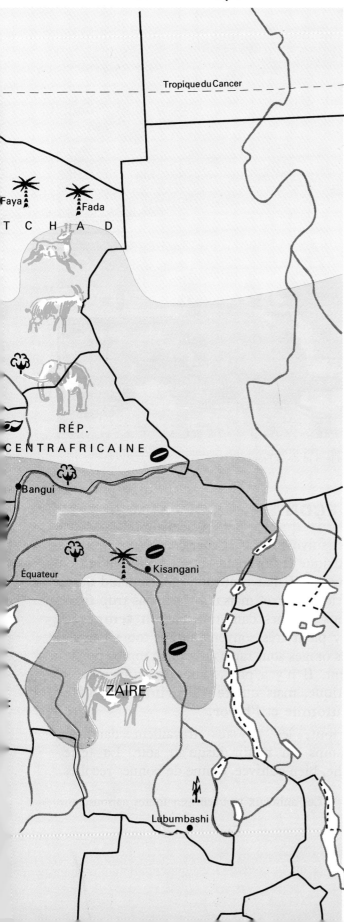

OBSERVONS

La carte situe les différents paysages de l'Afrique que nous venons d'étudier. La forêt est indiquée en gris, la savane en bistre foncé et le désert en bistre clair.

Cherchons l'Équateur. D'une manière générale, la forêt est proche de l'Équateur. A mesure que nous nous en éloignons, nous trouvons la savane puis, tout à fait au nord, le désert.

Quels arbres poussent dans la forêt ? dans les plantations ?

Que cultive-t-on dans les clairières ? Trouve-t-on beaucoup d'animaux dans la forêt ?

Quelles plantes poussent dans la savane ?

Quels sont les animaux domestiques de la savane ? Montrons sur la carte et nommons les animaux sauvages que l'on chasse dans cette région.

Quel est l'animal du désert ? Montrons-le sur la carte.

QUESTIONS ET EXERCICES

Sur une carte de l'Afrique Noire, plaçons l'Équateur. Essayons ensuite de situer les pays de forêt, de savane, puis le désert.

Colorions en vert les régions de forêts, en marron les régions de savane, puis en jaune le désert. Citons des pays de forêts, des pays de savane, des pays de désert.

53

Photo L. de Selva/Hoa-Qui.

Fig. 1 - Travaux des champs dans le Sud de la France.

OBSERVONS

Les documents : Sur la *figure 1*, nous voyons des **hommes** qui ne nous ressemblent pas. Sont-ils habillés comme nous ? Pourquoi ? Que font-ils ?

Les **maisons** de la *figure 2* ressemblent-elles aux nôtres ? Avec quels matériaux sont-elles faites ? Pourquoi ? Connaissons-nous les arbres ? Sont-ils plus grands ou plus petits que ceux de notre pays ?

LEÇON

Poursuivons notre voyage. Nous quittons l'Afrique et un grand bateau nous conduit en **Europe.** Il fait beaucoup moins chaud qu'en Afrique Noire, mais il n'y fait pas trop froid. Nous sommes dans une **région tempérée.** Il y pleut très souvent durant toute l'année. Les orages sont rares et la pluie tombe doucement. Il n'y a plus deux saisons, comme en Afrique, mais quatre : le **printemps, l'été, l'automne** et l'**hiver.**

Partout, les paysans travaillent dans les champs du matin jusqu'au soir. La terre, riche, bien cultivée, donne de bonnes récoltes.

Les animaux trouvent, en toutes saisons, une

Photo Combier.

Fig. 2 - Un village dans une région bien cultivée au Sud de Paris.

nourriture abondante dans les prairies. Le soir et quand il fait froid, on les rentre dans les étables ou dans les écuries. Ils sont toujours bien gras.

Les **forêts** couvrent les pentes des montagnes et quelques régions où rien d'autre ne pourrait pousser.

Les habitants des pays tempérés ne sont pas habillés comme nous. Ils doivent se protéger de la pluie et, en hiver, du froid et de la neige.

Dans les campagnes, les hommes vivent dans des maisons en pierre, couvertes d'ardoises ou de tuiles. Ils se groupent en **villages** qui sont entourés de leurs champs. Souvent, les hommes vivent dans de grandes **villes** et travaillent dans des bureaux ou des usines.

QUESTIONS ET EXERCICES

Cherchons dans un calendrier, les dates des saisons dans les pays tempérés. Quand commencent le printemps, l'été, l'automne, l'hiver ?

Recherchons des gravures représentant l'habillement, l'habitation et les travaux des hommes dans les pays tempérés.

Cherchons, sur le globe terrestre, les deux zones tempérées.

Dans ces zones tempérées, cherchons les noms des pays dont nous avons entendu parler.

RÉSUMÉ

L'Europe se trouve dans la zone tempérée. Il n'y fait ni trop chaud ni trop froid. Les pays tempérés ont 4 saisons : le printemps, l'été, l'automne et l'hiver.
Les hommes cultivent leurs champs ou travaillent dans des bureaux ou des usines.

Fig. 1 - Le long de la côte du Groenland, un bateau a du mal
à avancer au milieu des blocs de glace.

OBSERVONS

Les documents : Dans quel pays sommes-nous ? Que voyons-nous sur le sol ? De quoi la mer est-elle recouverte *(figure 1)* ?

Regardez la *figure 2*. Les **hommes** sont-ils habillés comme nous ? De quoi sont faits leurs vêtements ? Pourquoi ?

Les **animaux** que nous voyons sur la *figure 2* sont des rennes. Ces animaux vivent-ils aussi dans notre pays ? Comment appelle-t-on la voiture à laquelle ils sont attelés ?

LEÇON

Nous avons poursuivi notre long voyage et un nouveau bateau nous conduit très loin vers le **Nord.**

Nous **approchons du pôle Nord.** Il fait de plus en plus froid.

Notre bateau a de plus en plus de mal à avancer, car la mer est couverte de gros blocs de **glace.**

Lorsque nous touchons la terre, nous voyons qu'elle est tout entière recouverte d'une épaisse couche de neige durcie.

Comme il fait froid ! Le soleil, très pâle, s'élève à peine au-dessus de l'horizon. Le thermomètre est beaucoup descendu et indique une température au-dessous de zéro.

Fig. 2 - Près de son habitation, faite de blocs de glace,
une famille d'Esquimaux et son troupeau de rennes.

Nous n'aimerions pas vivre dans ces pays et pourtant des hommes y habitent. Ils ne sont pas nombreux. On les appelle des **Esquimaux.**

Ils vivent dans de petites maisons creusées dans la terre gelée et couvertes de blocs taillés dans la glace.

Ils ne peuvent pas cultiver la terre qui est toujours couverte de neige et de glace.

Ils chassent les **rennes** et les **phoques** et se nourrissent de leur viande, de leur graisse et de leur huile.

Avec la peau des rennes, les Esquimaux font des vêtements chauds. Ils circulent sur la neige gelée dans des **traîneaux** tirés par des rennes. Ils naviguent sur la mer dans des **pirogues** légères en peau de phoque.

QUESTIONS ET EXERCICES

Cherchons sur le globe terrestre où se trouvent situés les pays froids auprès du Pôle Nord et du Pôle Sud.

Comment appelle-t-on les habitants de ces pays?
De quoi sont-ils habillés? Pourquoi? Comment construisent-ils leurs maisons? De quoi se nourrissent-ils?

Comment se déplacent-ils sur terre? sur mer?

RÉSUMÉ

Près des pôles, au Nord et au Sud des pays tempérés, se trouvent des pays froids. La mer y est souvent gelée. La terre est couverte d'une épaisse couche de neige durcie. Vêtus de peaux de bêtes, les Esquimaux chassent les rennes et les phoques.

Photo Naud/AAA-Photo.

Fig. 1 - Jeune enfant maure.

Fig. 2 - Jeune fille peule.

OBSERVONS

Autour de nous : Les habitants de notre village sont-ils tous de la même race ? Y a-t-il des étrangers dans notre village ? De quelles races sont-ils ?

Les documents : Ils représentent des habitants de l'Afrique Noire. Se ressemblent-ils ? Qu'est-ce qui les différencie ? De quelles races sont-ils ? Quelles langues parlent-ils ? Dans quelles régions et dans quels pays habitent-ils ?

LEÇON

Tous les habitants de l'Afrique Noire ne se ressemblent pas, comme le prouvent les photographies ci-dessus.

L'un a la peau presque blanche ; les autres sont noirs, mais différents quand même les uns des autres. Il en est de même, parfois, des habitants d'un même village. Ils ne sont pas de la même **race** ou de la même **ethnie**. Si nous ne tenons pas compte des Européens, des Libanais et des Syriens, venus d'autres pays, les habitants de **race blanche** sont peu nombreux en Afrique Noire. Ils vivent aux limites du désert et de la savane. Ce sont les **Maures**, les **Touaregs** et les **Arabes**.

Les **Peuls** sont aussi de race blanche, mais leur peau est beaucoup moins claire.

Photo Vincent/AAA-Photo.
Fig. 3 - Femme Ouolof.

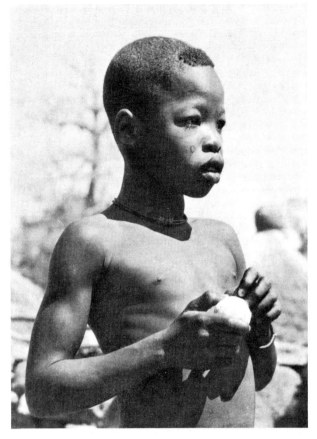
Fig. 4 - Garçon du Bénin.

Pasteurs et éleveurs, on les rencontre gardant leurs troupeaux dans toute l'Afrique Noire.

Les **Noirs** sont les plus nombreux, mais tous ne se ressemblent pas. Ils ne parlent pas la même langue et souvent n'ont pas la même religion. Ils sont de races différentes et ces races sont très nombreuses.

Les plus importantes sont :
— En Afrique Occidentale : les **Ouolofs**, les **Malinkés**, les **Mossis**, les **Haoussas**, les **Bambaras**, les **Yoroubas**, les **Akans**, les **Krous**.
— En Afrique Centrale : les **Négrilles**, les **Saras**, les **Bantous**, parmi lesquels on distingue encore des multitudes de petites ethnies.
— A Madagascar, les **Mérinas** et les **Betsiléos**.

QUESTIONS ET EXERCICES

De quelles races sont les habitants de notre village ? Quelle est la race la plus nombreuse ?

Notre race : *les hommes sont-ils petits ou grands ? Sont-ils cultivateurs, éleveurs ou artisans ? Portent-ils un costume particulier ?*
Y a-t-il des étrangers au village ? De quelle race sont-ils ? D'où viennent-ils ? Que font-ils au village ?

RÉSUMÉ

Tous les habitants de l'Afrique Noire ne sont pas de la même race. Les Maures, les Touaregs, les Arabes et les Peuls sont de race blanche. Les races noires les plus nombreuses sont les Ouolofs, les Malinkés, les Mossis, les Bambaras, les Négrilles, les Bantous et les Saras.

Fig. 1 - Enfants noirs.

Photo Dominique Buigné

Fig. 2 - Enfants blancs.

OBSERVONS

Autour de nous : Y a-t-il dans notre village ou à la ville voisine, des étrangers à l'Afrique. De quelles races sont-ils ?

Les documents : Ils représentent des enfants des différentes parties du monde.

Les uns *(figure 1)* sont noirs comme nous. Les autres sont blancs *(figure 2)* comme les Européens de la ville. Les enfants de la *figure 3* ont la peau jaune. La mère et sa petite fille de la *figure 4* ont la peau cuivrée, presque rouge.

LEÇON

Nous avons vu, dans la dernière leçon, qu'il y avait en Afrique des habitants de races différentes. Ce qui est vrai en Afrique est encore beaucoup plus visible si nous voyageons à travers le monde. On y rencontre des Noirs, des Blancs, des Jaunes et même des hommes à la peau cuivrée.

La **race blanche** est présente partout dans le monde, mais surtout dans les **pays tempérés**. Les **Européens** sont des hommes de race blanche.

Les hommes de **race jaune** habitent en **Asie**, en **Chine**, au **Japon**. Les habitants de ces pays ont la peau jaune. Ils ont les cheveux noirs, raides et les yeux bridés.

Photo Ergi Landau.

Fig. 3 - Enfants jaunes.

Photo Ursula Bagel.

Fig. 4 - Peaux-Rouges.

Ils sont, en général, de petite taille. Ils se nourrissent surtout de riz et de poisson.

La **race noire** est la race des régions chaudes du globe. On la rencontre surtout en Afrique, mais aussi en **Asie** et en **Amérique.**

Les Noirs américains, de plus en plus nombreux, sont les descendants des anciens esclaves achetés en Afrique.

La **race rouge** est la moins importante de toutes. Elle peuplait à l'origine le **continent américain.** Les membres de cette race ont la peau cuivrée, et les cheveux très noirs. On les appelle **Peaux-Rouges** ou **Indiens.**

Les conquérants blancs les ont massacrés au siècle dernier. Les descendants des survivants vivent aux Etats-Unis et au Canada.

QUESTIONS ET EXERCICES

Dans quelles régions du monde rencontre-t-on des Blancs, des Jaunes, des Noirs, des Peaux-Rouges ?

Quelle est la race la plus nombreuse du globe ? la moins nombreuse ?

Recherchons sur le globe les régions où vivent ces différentes races.

RÉSUMÉ

Tous les hommes qui vivent sur la terre ne se ressemblent pas. Ils sont de races différentes. Les Blancs vivent surtout dans les pays tempérés.
Les Jaunes peuplent les pays chauds de l'Asie.
On rencontre des Noirs dans les régions chaudes d'Afrique et d'Amérique. Les Peaux-Rouges vivent en Amérique.

Fig. 1 - Tente maure.

Photo Hoa-Qui.

Fig. 2 - Dans un village de la savane.

Photo Hoa-Qui.

OBSERVONS

Autour de nous : Les habitations de notre village. Comment les construit-on ? Avec quels matériaux ? Sont-elles toutes construites sur le même modèle ?
Dessinons, puis décrivons notre maison.

Les documents : Que représentent-ils ? Y retrouvons-nous des habitations de notre pays ? Se ressemblent-elles ? Pourquoi ?
Décrivons-les une à une, et cherchons, d'après la photographie, en quels matériaux elles sont faites.

LEÇON

En **Afrique Noire,** tous les habitants vivent dans des **maisons.** Mais toutes ces maisons ne se ressemblent pas.

Dans le **désert,** il ne pleut presque pas. On n'y trouve ni eau, ni paille, ni bois. Les habitants qui se déplacent souvent ne construisent pas de maisons. Ils vivent sous des **tentes** en laine ou en poil de chameau *(figure 1)*.

Dans le **nord de la savane,** il pleut rarement. Les habitations sont construites en **banco** et leur toit est plat *(figure 2)*.

Dans la **forêt,** il pleut beaucoup. Les maisons sont rondes, aux murs en banco ou en branchages. La toiture, pointue, est faite de paille, de feuilles ou de palmes *(figure 3)*.

Photo Hoa-Qui.

Fig. 3 - Dans un village de la forêt.

Fig. 4 - Habitations sur pilotis.

Dans certaines montagnes, le paysan doit lutter contre la pluie mais surtout contre le froid. Le toit, en paille, descend presque jusqu'à terre.

Dans certaines **régions humides** les habitations sont construites au-dessus de l'eau, sur des **pilotis** *(figure 4)*.

Toutes ces habitations ne comprennent, en général, qu'une seule pièce où vit toute la famille.

De plus en plus, dans les petites villes et même dans les villages de brousse, les Africains habitent des maisons en dur, construites en briques ou en parpaings et couvertes de tôles ou de tuiles.

Ces maisons comprennent plusieurs pièces et sont souvent confortables.

QUESTIONS ET EXERCICES

Observons une maison de notre village. En quels matériaux est-elle construite ? Faites-en le plan, puis dessinez-la exactement comme vous la voyez.

Y a-t-il, dans notre région, des maisons qui ne ressemblent pas aux nôtres ? Décrivons-les et dessinons-les.

Cherchons des gravures représentant des habitations d'Afrique Noire.

RÉSUMÉ

Les habitants des régions sèches d'Afrique Noire vivent sous la tente ou dans des maisons en banco aux toits plats. Dans les régions pluvieuses, les maisons sont couvertes de paille ou de feuilles. Le toit descend parfois jusqu'au sol.

Fig. 1 - Dans les champs, les paysans labourent et sèment.
D'autres habitants du village pêchent dans la rivière.

OBSERVONS

Autour de nous : Que font, en général, les habitants de notre village ? Notons leurs occupations en saison sèche, en saison des pluies.

Les documents : Que représentent-ils ? Sur la *figure 1*, les paysans travaillent aux champs. Que font-ils ? En quelle saison se font ces travaux ?
Que font les femmes sur la *figure 2 ?* A quel travail se livre l'artisan installé sur la place du village ?

LEÇON

Mon village n'est pas bien grand. Il a ... habitants. Presque tous les habitants de mon village sont des **cultivateurs.**

Tout autour de leur maison, ils cultivent du manioc, de la patate, du coton, des tarots. En dehors du village, ils ont des champs d'arachides, de mil, de riz ou de fonio.

Certains, parmi eux, **élèvent des bœufs,** des moutons, des chèvres, quelques poules et, quelquefois, des porcs.

Hommes, femmes et enfants travaillent aux champs au moment des cultures.

D'autres habitants des villages près du fleuve

Fig. 2 - Au village, les femmes pilent le mil pour préparer le repas.
Le tisserand travaille. Les enfants jouent.

se livrent à **la pêche.** D'autres encore, en même temps qu'ils cultivent leur champ, sont forgerons, tisserands, cordonniers, etc. Ce sont des **artisans.**

Sous une petite case, un **commerçant** vend du sel, du sucre, du pétrole, des allumettes. Il achète les produits du pays.

Nous l'appelons « un balancier » car il a une grande balance pour peser ces produits.

En saison sèche, lorsque les graines sont rentrées, il n'y a plus beaucoup de travail : on refait les maisons, on voyage, et, tous les soirs, on danse au son du tam-tam. Mais, dès les premières pluies, la campagne s'anime. Tout le monde est aux champs. C'est la saison des cultures.

QUESTIONS ET EXERCICES

Quels sont, dans notre village, les travaux de saison sèche, d'hivernage?
Retraçons, pour une journée, l'emploi du temps de notre père, de notre mère.
Quels sont les animaux élevés dans notre village?
Y a-t-il beaucoup d'artisans au village? Que font-ils? Comment les appelle-t-on?
Quelles sont les principales fêtes au village?

RÉSUMÉ

Mon village s'appelle ... Il a ... habitants. Presque tous les habitants de mon village sont des cultivateurs. Quelques-uns élèvent des animaux. Mais on y rencontre aussi des artisans : ..., ..., ... et un commerçant.

31 L'AGRICULTURE EN AFRIQUE

Fig. 1 - Le défrichage à la machette.

AAA-Photo.

Fig. 2 - Le travail à la daba.

OBSERVONS

Autour de nous : Observons des cultivateurs au travail. Comment labourent-ils le sol ? Avec quels instruments ? Quels produits récoltent-ils ? Quand ? Comment ?

Les documents : Ils nous montrent des paysans africains au travail. A quels travaux se livrent-ils ? Dessinons les outils qu'ils utilisent.
Quelles sont les principales cultures de notre village, de notre région ?

LEÇON

Les photographies nous montrent des **paysans** africains au travail. Sur la *figure 1*, nous les voyons couper des branches et des herbes avec leur **machette** et les brûler. Puis ils répandront les cendres sur le sol qui sera retourné avec la houe ou la **daba** *(figure 2)*.

Ces travaux sont pénibles et n'avancent pas vite.

La *figure 3* nous montre le travail au **tracteur.** Le paysan répand de l'engrais dans un champ.

Avec son tracteur, il peut labourer beaucoup plus vite et préparer de plus grandes surfaces, avec moins de fatigue.

Photo B. François/Hoa-Qui.

Fig. 3 - Epandage d'engrais au tracteur (Côte-d'Ivoire).

Ces tracteurs permettent de labourer, en une journée, d'immenses étendues. Mais le paysan pourrait finir par épuiser le sol de son champ. Il doit alors utiliser des engrais.

Souvent les récoltes sont faites à la machette ou à la faucille, mais aussi avec des **moissonneuses**.

Dans certaines régions riches, les Européens, vite imités par certains paysans africains, ont établi des **plantations.** Ils ont défriché le sol. Ils l'assèchent ou l'arrosent. Ils l'enrichissent avec des engrais.

Le paysan africaïn cultive surtout l'arachide, le riz, le mil, le manioc, l'igname, le fonio. Les plantations produisents des bananes, du café, du cacao, des ananas, qui, récoltés avec beaucoup de soins, sont expédiés dans le monde entier.

QUESTIONS ET EXERCICES

Comment les paysans de notre village cultivent-ils le sol? Avec quels outils?

Pendant combien d'années labourent-ils le même terrain?

Quelles sont les principales cultures de notre région?

Existe-t-il des plantations dans notre région? Occupent-elles beaucoup d'employés? Que produisent-elles?

RÉSUMÉ

Le paysan africain travaille le sol à l'aide d'une daba et parfois avec une charrue ou un tracteur. Il cultive l'arachide, le mil, le riz, le manioc, l'igname.
Les riches plantations d'Afrique Noire produisent du café, du cacao et des fruits.

32 L'ÉLEVAGE EN AFRIQUE

Photo Naud/AAA-Photo.

Fig. 1 - Un troupeau de chameaux s'abreuve à un puits, en Mauritanie.

OBSERVONS

Autour de nous : Quelles sont les bêtes élevées dans notre village ? Où vivent-elles, le jour, la nuit ? Par qui sont-elles gardées ? A quoi servent-elles ? Sont-elles employées par l'homme pour l'aider dans ses travaux ? Lesquelles ?

Les documents : Dans quelles régions sommes-nous ? Quels animaux y reconnaissons-nous ? Sont-ils bien gardés et bien soignés par les paysans ?

LEÇON

Beaucoup de paysans d'Afrique Noire sont des cultivateurs, mais presque tous aussi élèvent des animaux.

Les animaux élevés varient suivant la région. Le **chameau** est l'animal du **désert** *(figure 1)* où l'on rencontre aussi des troupeaux de moutons et de chèvres.

La **savane** est la **grande région d'élevage** de l'Afrique Noire. On y élève des moutons, des zébus ou **bœufs** à bosse dans le Nord *(figure 2)*, des bœufs plus petits et sans bosse dans le Sud. Le **cheval** est un animal de la savane. La **volaille** (poules, canards, pintades) vit autour de la case et aussi, de

Photo Naud/AAA-Photo.

Fig. 2 - Un troupeau de zébus vient boire dans le fleuve Niger.

plus en plus, dans de beaux poulaillers. Les pays humides du Sud élèvent plutôt des **porcs** et des **poulets**.

L'éleveur africain aime beaucoup ses bêtes, mais les soigne peu. Souvent, les troupeaux vivent à la belle étoile et se nourrissent tout seuls. C'est pourquoi, en hivernage, les bêtes sont grasses et bien portantes. Pendant la saison sèche, au contraire, elles sont maigres et doivent chercher leur pâture loin du village. Elles sont alors quelquefois victimes des bêtes sauvages.

Les chameaux, les chevaux et les bœufs portent de lourdes charges ou les traînent dans des charrettes. Les animaux nous donnent la viande, le lait, les œufs, le cuir et la laine.

QUESTIONS ET EXERCICES

Quels animaux les paysans de notre village élèvent-ils ? Où vivent ces bêtes en hivernage ? en saison sèche ? Qui les garde ? Qui leur donne leur nourriture ?

A quoi servent ces animaux dans notre village ? Pour quels travaux aident-ils le paysan ? Quels aliments nous donnent-ils ? Mesurez la quantité de lait donnée par une vache, en hivernage, en saison sèche.

RÉSUMÉ

L'Afrique Noire possède, dans ses diverses régions, des troupeaux de chameaux, de bœufs, de moutons et de chèvres. On y élève aussi des chevaux, des porcs et de la volaille.
Ces animaux nous donnent leur travail et aussi de la viande, du lait, des œufs, du cuir et de la laine.

69

Fig. 1 - Un tisserand.

Photo Almasy.

Fig. 2 - Un forgeron.

OBSERVONS

Autour de nous : Observons les artisans de notre village au travail. Sont-ils nombreux ? Où travaillent-ils ? Quels objets fabriquent-ils ? Dessinons-les. Quels sont leurs outils ? Dessinons-les. Quels matériaux emploient-ils ?

Les documents : Ils représentent des artisans africains au travail. Où travaillent-ils ? Que font-ils ? Quels objets fabriquent-ils ? De quels outils se servent-ils ?

LEÇON

Dans presque tous les petits villages d'Afrique, on peut voir des **artisans** au travail. On y rencontre des **tisserands**, des **forgerons**, des **cordonniers** et des **potiers**. Ils vivent au village comme tout le monde mais, parfois, ils se groupent en coopérative.

Assis à l'ombre d'un arbre, le **tisserand** *(figure 1)* tisse le fil de coton que les femmes ont filé. Il fabrique des bandes de tissu.

Le **forgeron** *(figure 2)* travaille dans la forge, près du feu. Il fabrique ou répare les instruments agricoles, les bicyclettes et même parfois les automobiles. Les **bijoutiers** fabriquent de beaux bijoux en or ou en argent.

Photo Naud/AAA-Photo.

Fig. 3 - Une potière.

Photo Naud/AAA-Photo.

Fig. 4 - Un artisan sculptant le bois.

Le **cordonnier** tanne les peaux et en fait des chaussures, des sacs, des selles. C'est lui aussi qui fabrique les amulettes et les gris-gris. Le **potier** fait des canaris de toutes formes et de toutes tailles et des gargoulettes *(figure 3)*.

A la petite ville voisine nous connaissons d'autres artisans. Les **maçons** bâtissent des maisons. Les **menuisiers** font des tables pour les écoles et des meubles. Sur le seuil des boutiques, les **tailleurs** cousent, à la machine, de beaux vêtements.

Dans les villes, des **garages** se sont installés. Des **mécaniciens** y réparent les automobiles, les motos et les cyclomoteurs.

Souvent, ces artisans travaillent seuls ou avec un apprenti. Leur **atelier** est modeste et leur outillage assez simple.

QUESTIONS ET EXERCICES

Y a-t-il beaucoup d'artisans dans notre village ?
Quels métiers exercent-ils ? Quels sont les plus nombreux ?
Travaillent-ils au village même ? Où ? Certains d'entre eux sont-ils groupés dans une coopérative ? Lesquels ?
Essayons de dessiner leur atelier, leurs outils, les objets qu'ils fabriquent.
Où et à qui vendent-ils ces objets ?

RÉSUMÉ

Tous les habitants de notre village ne sont pas des cultivateurs. On y rencontre aussi des artisans comme le tisserand, le forgeron, le cordonnier, le potier, le maçon, le menuisier et le mécanicien.

34 LA PÊCHE EN AFRIQUE NOIRE

Fig. 1 - Avec leur filet, ces pêcheurs vont aller capturer des poissons.

OBSERVONS

Autour de nous : La pêche et la chasse se pratiquent-elles dans notre région?

Qui pratique la pêche? Où? A l'aide de quels instruments? Quels poissons pêche-t-on?

Qui se livre à la chasse? Où? De quelles armes se sert-on?

Les documents: Que représentent-ils? Quels instruments de pêche voyons-nous sur la *figure 1*?

Quel instrument de chasse utilise-t-on sur la *figure 2*?

LEÇON

Dans les rivières, les lacs et surtout au bord de la mer, les habitants de l'Afrique Noire se livrent à la **pêche.**

Dans les rivières, les **pêcheurs** se servent de **lignes,** de **nasses,** de **filets** ou même de **harpons.** Dans certaines régions la pêche en eau douce, dans les rivières et dans les lacs, donne lieu à de grandes fêtes.

Tout le long des côtes, les pêcheurs capturent le poisson. Ils se servent de **lignes,** traînées derrière leurs pirogues, et de **filets.** De plus en plus, les pêcheurs africains traînent derrière de grands bateaux à moteur, d'immenses filets qu'on appelle des **chaluts.**

Photo Huet Hoa-Qui.
Fig. 2 - Chasse au filet en forêt (Centrafrique).

Photo M. Renaudeau/Hoa-Qui.
Fig. 3 - Chasse au fusil en savane (Sénégal).

Une grande partie du poisson capturé est mangée sur place ou vendue au marché voisin. Mais une autre partie de ce poisson est **séchée, fumée,** mise en **conserve** dans des usines, puis expédiée vers les États de l'intérieur ou même vers les pays lointains.

Dans les régions de savane, les bêtes sauvages sont nombreuses et les paysans pratiquent la **chasse** *(figure 3)*. Ils chassent des **antilopes** et des **biches.** Le **lion,** la **panthère,** l'**éléphant,** longtemps chassés sans contrôle, sont maintenant protégés afin d'éviter leur disparition.

On chasse encore avec des **flèches** et des **sagaies** mais, de plus en plus, au **fusil.**

La chasse apporte de la viande à tous les habitants du village.

QUESTIONS ET EXERCICES

Comment pratique-t-on la pêche dans notre région ? Quels sont les bateaux et les instruments utilisés ? Dessinons-les.

Quelles sortes de poissons pêche-t-on ? Que fait-on du poisson pêché ?

Quels animaux chasse-t-on dans notre région ? Qui les chasse ? Avec quelles armes ? A quoi servent les bêtes tuées ?

RÉSUMÉ

En Afrique Noire, les habitants se livrent à la pêche le long des fleuves, au bord des lacs et au bord de la mer. Ils pêchent à la ligne, à la nasse, au filet et au chalut.
Les régions de savane sont des grandes régions de chasse.

73

35 LE MARCHÉ DE MON VILLAGE

Fig. 1 - Jour de marché, au village.

OBSERVONS

Autour de nous : Promenons-nous au marché du village et notons tout ce que nous voyons.
Allons voir une boutique. Essayons de dresser une liste de tous les objets qui y sont achetés ou vendus.

Les documents : La *figure 1* représente un marché de village. Où sont installés les marchands ? Que vendent-ils ? La *figure 2* nous montre l'intérieur d'une boutique. Quelles marchandises y voyons-nous ?

LEÇON

Le **marché** se tient tous les jeudis, sur une petite colline, à côté de notre village. C'est un **marché hebdomadaire.**

Les paysans, qui viennent de tous les villages alentour, apportent sur leur tête tous les produits qu'ils veulent vendre.

Les **dioulas** de la ville voisine viennent en camions. Ils déballent leurs marchandises sur des nattes à l'ombre des manguiers. Dans un coin, des **potiers** vendent des canaris ; le **forgeron** vend des dabas et des machettes. Plus loin, le **boucher** dépèce une vache.

Les habitants de mon village vendent au marché les produits de leurs récoltes.

74

Fig. 2 - Dans la boutique du village.

Au chef-lieu du département, la place du marché est entourée de **boutiques.** Sous les vérandas, s'entassent des fûts, des sacs de riz et de manioc et une grande bascule. Sur le pas de sa porte, un **tailleur** coud de beaux boubous.

La **boutique** est divisée en deux par un long **comptoir.** D'un côté, les **acheteurs** s'empressent. De l'autre, le **gérant** et ses employés vendent des marchandises et écrivent sur des registres.

On trouve de tout dans ces boutiques : des produits alimentaires, des ustensiles de cuisine, des étoffes, des dabas, des machettes. Ces marchandises sont bien disposées sur des étagères ou suspendues au plafond ou à une longue corde.

QUESTIONS ET EXERCICES

Où se tient le marché de notre village ? Quand a-t-il lieu ? Que vend-on au marché, en hivernage ? en saison sèche ? Qui vend ? D'où viennent ces vendeurs ? Comment transportent-ils leurs marchandises ? Viennent-ils régulièrement ?

Combien y a-t-il de boutiques au chef-lieu de notre département ? Qui tient ces boutiques ?

Que peut-on y acheter ? D'où viennent ces produits ?

RÉSUMÉ

Le marché de mon village a lieu le ... On y vend ... On peut y acheter d... Dans la boutique, je peux acheter des aliments, des étoffes, des vêtements, des ustensiles de cuisine et les outils dont le cultivateur a besoin.

36 LA VIE A LA VILLE

Fig. 1 - Vue générale de Libreville (Gabon).

Photo M. Renaudeau/Hoa-Qui.

OBSERVONS

Autour de nous : Y a-t-il une grande ville dans notre pays ? Cherchons un plan de cette ville et des photographies. Sur le plan, suivons du doigt une rue. Ressemble-t-elle aux sentiers d'un village ?

Les documents : Ce sont des photographies aériennes de Libreville et d'Abidjan. Y voyons-nous des maisons comme dans notre village ? Comptons les étages des plus hautes maisons.

LEÇON

Pendant les grandes vacances, Mamadou est allé à Libreville. **Libreville** n'est pas un petit village, ni un chef-lieu de département. C'est la **capitale** du **Gabon** et une grande ville de l'Afrique Noire. Elle compte près de trois cent mille habitants.

A Libreville, on ne peut pas se promener n'importe où sur la route, ni traverser les rues où on veut ; on se ferait écraser par les nombreuses automobiles. Les **rues** sont larges, droites et goudronnées. Elles sont bordées de **trottoirs** sur lesquels marchent les piétons. De chaque côté des rues, se dressent de grandes maisons qui ont parfois plus de dix

Fig. 2 - Une vue d'Abidjan (Côte-d'Ivoire).

Photo M. Huet/Hoa-Qui.

étages et qu'on appelle des **immeubles.** Toutes les maisons sont construites en dur et il n'y a pas de cultures autour des habitations.

Mamadou a vu de grands et beaux **magasins** avec de larges **vitrines** bien garnies de produits de toutes sortes. Il a vu le palais du Président de la République, les immeubles administratifs, l'Assemblée nationale, le lycée, la mosquée et la cathédrale. Il a vu aussi de nombreux cinémas.

Il y a beaucoup de grandes villes en Afrique Noire : Nouakchott, Dakar, Saint-Louis, Bamako, Abidjan, Accra, Lomé, Ouagadougou, Conakry, Niamey, Cotonou, Lagos, Douala, Yaoundé, Brazzaville, Pointe-Noire, Libreville, Bangui, N'Djaména, Kinshasa, etc.

QUESTIONS ET EXERCICES

Recherchons des plans et des vues des villes de notre pays et des autres régions de l'Afrique Noire.

Comment s'appelle la ville voisine de notre village? Combien a-t-elle d'habitants? Comment y sont les rues? Comment se coupent-elles? Y a-t-il des grands magasins dans cette ville?

Essayons de placer sur une carte (voir p. 78) les grandes villes de notre pays et d'Afrique Noire.

RÉSUMÉ

Libreville est une grande ville de l'Afrique Noire. Les rues, droites, sont bordées de trottoirs et de hautes maisons à plusieurs étages. Toutes les maisons sont construites en dur.

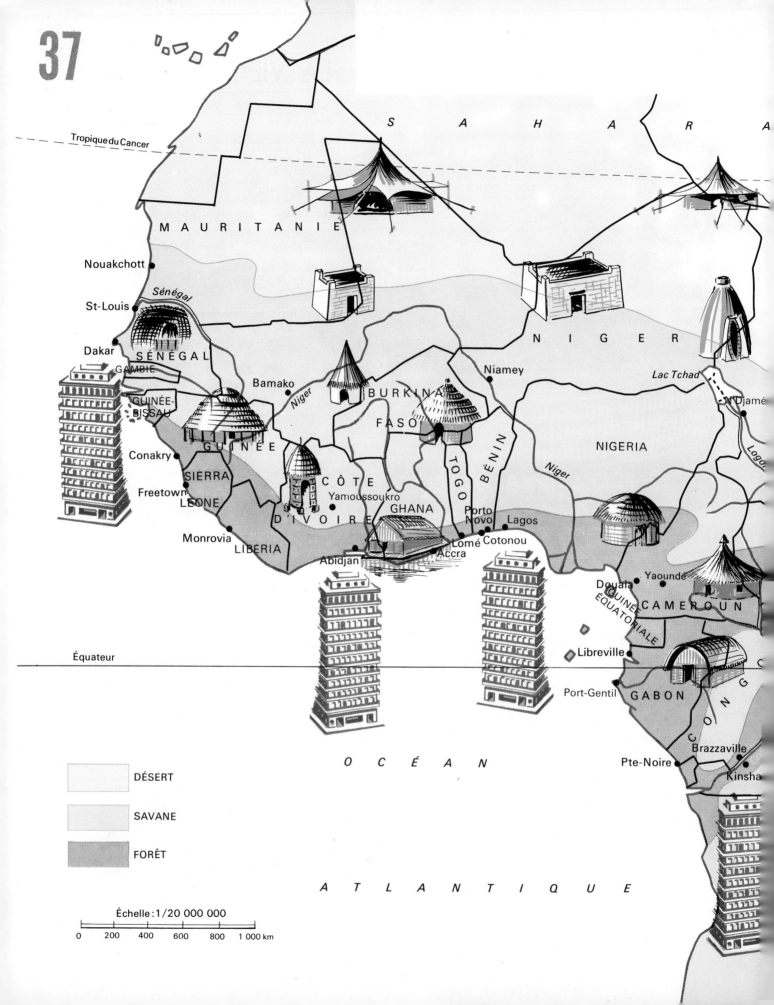

37

Tropique du Cancer

S A H A R A

M A U R I T A N I E

Nouakchott

Sénégal

St-Louis

Dakar

SÉNÉGAL

GAMBIE

GUINÉE-
BISSAU

Bamako

Niger

BURKINA

N I G E R

Niamey

Lac Tchad

N'Djamé

FASO

Conakry

GUINÉE

CÔTE

SIERRA

LEONE

Freetown

Yamoussoukro

D'IVOIRE

GHANA

TOGO

BÉNIN

Niger

NIGERIA

Porto
Novo

Lagos

Monrovia

LIBERIA

Abidjan

Lomé Cotonou

Accra

Yaoundé

Douala

CAMEROUN

GUINÉE
ÉQUATORIALE

Libreville

Port-Gentil

GABON

Équateur

C O N G O

Brazzaville

Pte-Noire

Kinsha

O C É A N

A T L A N T I Q U E

	DÉSERT
	SAVANE
	FORÊT

Échelle : 1/20 000 000

0   200   400   600   800   1 000 km

L'AFRIQUE NOIRE : HABITATIONS ET VILLES

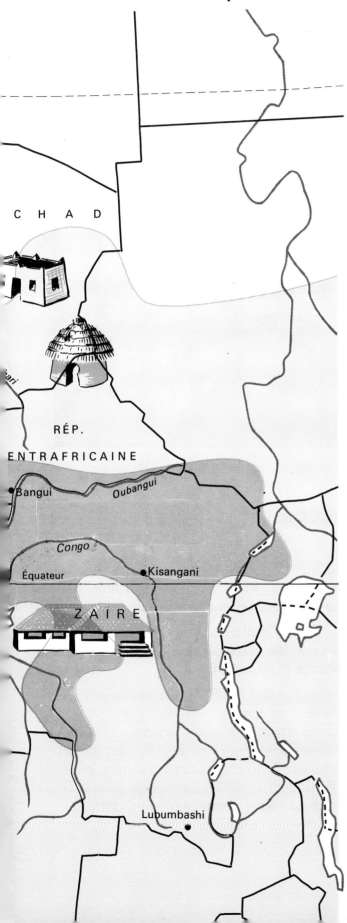

OBSERVONS

La carte nous montre les différentes habitations que l'on peut rencontrer en Afrique Noire. Elle nous apprend à situer les principales villes.

Dans le désert, où il ne pleut pas et où il n'y a ni bois, ni paille, ni eau, nous voyons les tentes. Nous en avons déjà vu sur la photographie p. 62, *figure 1*.

Au nord de la savane, où il ne pleut pas beaucoup, les maisons en banco ont les toits plats. Regardez de nouveau la photographie page 62, *figure 2*,

Plus au sud, les maisons en banco au toit pointu sont couvertes de paille.

Les habitations de montagne ont un toit qui descend presque jusqu'au sol pour protéger du froid.

En forêt, les toitures sont faites de feuilles d'arbres ou de palmes, comme sur la photographie page 63, *figure 3*.

Sur les lacs et près de la côte, certaines maisons sont construites sur pilotis, comme celles que vous avez vues sur la photographie, page 63, *figure 4*.

Les grandes villes sont de plus en plus nombreuses en Afrique Noire. Nommons-les. Montrons où elles sont situées. Dans ces villes on trouve des immeubles de plus en plus hauts.

Décrivez un immeuble en regardant ceux de la photographie de Libreville page 76.

QUESTIONS ET EXERCICES

Dessinons des petites maisons en prenant comme modèles celles que nous voyons sur la carte puis, en réfléchissant bien, amusons-nous à les placer sur une carte de l'Afrique Noire. Vérifions ensuite si elles sont bien placées.

Sur une carte muette, plaçons Abidjan, Lagos, Dakar, Kinshasa, Accra, Bamako, Niamey, Yaoudé, Brazzaville...

Jouons aux « noms de villes », comme nous l'avons fait pour les pays (v. p. 19).

Photo Hoa-Qui.

Fig. 1 - La chaîne de montage Renault-Automobiles à Abidjan (Côte-d'Ivoire).

OBSERVONS

Autour de nous : Existe-t-il des usines dans notre région? Qu'y fabrique-t-on? Combien y a-t-il d'ouvriers?

Visitons une usine avec notre maître et décrivons ce que nous avons vu.

Les documents : Ils représentent des usines d'Afrique Noire. Regardons *la figure 1*. C'est une usine de montage d'automobiles. Que produit la machine représentée sur la *figure 2* ?

LEÇON

Au cours des vacances, Koffi est allé à Abidjan. Il y a vu des artisans comme dans notre village ; mais il y a vu aussi beaucoup d'**ouvriers** qui se rendaient à leur **usine.**

Il a vu des **huileries,** une **cimenterie,** une **fabrique de chaussures,** une **usine de montage d'automobiles.**

Avec son oncle, Koffi a visité une usine. Les **ateliers,** immenses, sont dominés par de grandes cheminées qui fument. Plusieurs centaines d'ouvriers sont installés devant des machines. Ils font toujours les mêmes gestes et fabriquent toujours les mêmes pièces. Ils travaillent ainsi beaucoup plus vite que

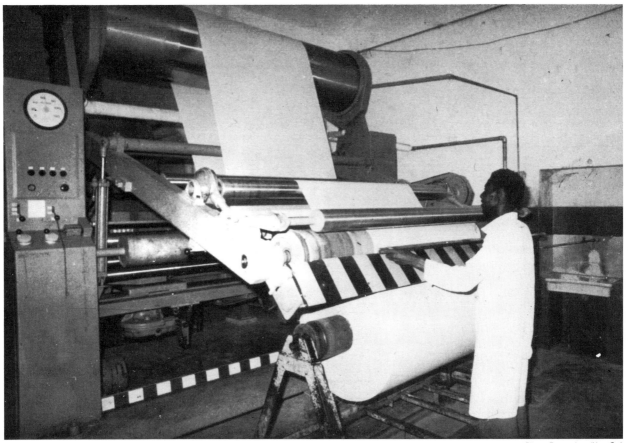

Fig. 2 - Dans une usine de tissage (Sénégal).

Photo Renaudeau/Hoa-Qui.

l'artisan du village. La *figure 1* nous montre une **usine de montage d'automobiles.** Le **châssis** avance automatiquement. Il passe devant des ouvriers qui y ajoutent toujours la même pièce. Cette forme de travail s'appelle le **travail à la chaîne.** Au bout de la chaîne, la voiture est prête à rouler et l'usine en monte plusieurs chaque jour.

Depuis l'Indépendance, de nombreuses usines se sont installées dans les États de l'Afrique Noire.

> On y trouve des **huileries,** des **brasseries,** des **filatures** et des **tissages,** des **raffineries de pétrole,** des **scieries** et des **fabriques de contre-plaqué,** des **fabriques** de **hangars métalliques** et des **usines de montage de cycles, d'automobiles** et de **camions.**

QUESTIONS ET EXERCICES

Existe-t-il des usines dans notre région ? Où sont-elles situées ? Que fabriquent-elles ? Combien ont-elles de machines ? Combien emploient-elles d'ouvriers ?

D'où viennent les matières employées à l'usine ? Où expédie-t-on les produits qui y sont fabriqués ?

Cherchons des gravures représentant des usines d'Afrique Noire.

RÉSUMÉ

Une usine est un vaste atelier qui emploie un grand nombre d'ouvriers travaillant avec des machines perfectionnées. Ils travaillent à la chaîne et fabriquent, très vite, les machines et les produits dont nous avons besoin.

39 LES ROUTES D'AFRIQUE

Photo M. Huet/Hoa-Qui.

Fig. 1 - Une piste dans la brousse.

Photo M. Huet/Hoa-Qui.

Fig. 2 - Une route moderne en ville.

OBSERVONS

Autour de nous : D'où vient la route de notre village ? Où va-t-elle ? Quelle est la voie ferrée la plus proche de notre village ? D'où vient-elle ? Où se termine-t-elle ? Quelle est la gare la plus proche ?

Les documents : La *figure 2* nous montre une route moderne en ville. Ressemble-t-elle à la route qui mène à notre village (*figure 1*) ? Sur la *figure 3*, nous voyons les quais d'une gare. Montrons la motrice diesel, les wagons, le quai. Que font les voyageurs ?

LEÇON

Pour aller d'un village à l'autre, nous empruntons des **pistes** ou des **sentiers** bien étroits. Pour aller de notre village au chef-lieu du département, nous avons une **route**. Elle est large, empierrée et **goudronnée**. Elle traverse les marigots sur des **ponts**. On passe le grand fleuve sur un **bac**. Piétons et cyclistes circulent sur la route, mais on y rencontre surtout des **automobiles** et de gros **camions**.

Les camions transportent des marchandises. Sur les grandes routes, les voyageurs circulent maintenant dans de grands **autocars**, très rapides et très confortables.

Au chef-lieu du département, Moussa est

Photo Drachoussof/AAA-Photo.

Fig. 3 - Une gare sur la ligne Abidjan - Ouagadougou.

entré dans la **gare**. Il a pris un **billet** pour Ouagadougou. Moussa est monté dans le **train**. Le train roule sur des **rails** en acier. La **motrice diesel** tire derrière elle de nombreux **wagons de voyageurs** et des **wagons de marchandises**.

Le train franchit les vallées et les rivières sur de grands ponts. Il croise une route à un **passage à niveau**. Le train **rapide** ne s'arrête pas, comme l'**omnibus,** à toutes les gares.

En approchant de Ouagadougou, Moussa a vu des **autorails** qui sont de grands autocars montés sur rails. Il a vu aussi des trains qui ne transportaient que des marchandises dans des wagons spéciaux, lourdement chargés.

QUESTIONS ET EXERCICES

Les pistes, les sentiers et les routes de mon village. D'où viennent-ils? Où vont-ils? Avez-vous vu des ponts? Avec quels matériaux étaient-ils construits?

Faisons la carte des pistes et des sentiers autour de notre village.

Comment s'appellent la voie ferrée, la gare la plus proche de notre village? Combien y passe-t-il de trains par jour ou par semaine. S'arrêtent-ils tous à la gare? D'où viennent-ils? Où vont-ils? Que transportent-ils?

RÉSUMÉ

Des pistes et des sentiers relient entre eux les villages de brousse. Les grandes villes sont reliées par des routes goudronnées. Le chemin de fer relie les grandes villes de l'intérieur aux ports. Des trains rapides et des trains de marchandises y circulent.

Photo M. Renaudeau/Hoa-Qui.

Fig. 1 - Un paquebot à quai dans le port de Dakar (Sénégal).

OBSERVONS

Autour de nous : Si nous habitons au bord de la mer, connaissons-nous un port dans notre région ? Reçoit-il de gros bateaux ? D'où viennent-ils ? Quelles marchandises apportent-ils ?

Les documents : La *figure 1* nous montre un grand bateau à quai. Montrons les mâts, les cheminées.

La *figure 2* nous montre un grand port, le port de Douala. Cherchons les quais, les hangars, les bateaux.

LEÇON

Les **bateaux** viennent chercher un **abri** dans les **baies** de la côte. Un tel abri, bien aménagé, s'appelle un **port**.

Les petits ports reçoivent seulement les pirogues des pêcheurs. Les grands bateaux ne peuvent y accoster. Pour leur permettre d'aborder, on a construit une **jetée** en bois ou en ciment qui s'avance dans la mer et qu'on appelle un **wharf.** Dans les grands ports, des **quais** en pierre et en ciment remplacent le wharf.

Des camions et des trains y circulent pour amener aux bateaux de lourdes marchandises. Les bateaux sont chargés et déchargés à l'aide de **grues.**

Fig. 2 - Le grand port du Cameroun : Douala.

Boulbinet, à côté de Conakry, est un **port de pêche**. Il y a un **wharf** à **Port-Bouet**, à **Cotonou** et à **Lomé**. Pointe-Noire, Libreville, Port-Gentil, Douala, Cotonou, Abidjan et **Dakar** sont des **ports de commerce**.

Sur la *figure 2*, nous voyons, le long des quais, des bateaux qui transportent des marchandises : ce sont des **cargos**. De puissantes machines font tourner une **hélice** qui fait avancer le bateau. A l'avant et à l'arrière, le cargo possède un ou deux **mâts** solides qui servent à décharger la cargaison.

Certains cargos, spécialement aménagés, transportent des minerais : ce sont des **minéraliers**. Un bateau qui transporte des centaines de passagers est un **paquebot**.

QUESTIONS ET EXERCICES

Notre pays a-t-il des ports? Lesquels? A-t-il un wharf? Quels bateaux y accostent? D'où viennent-ils? Que chargent-ils dans nos ports? Que déchargent-ils?
Cherchons des gravures de bateaux.

Plaçons sur notre carte les grands ports de l'Afrique Noire. Cherchons à savoir quelles sont les marchandises qu'on y charge et qu'on y décharge.

RÉSUMÉ

Un abri pour les bateaux est un port. Un wharf est une jetée qui s'avance dans la mer et permet aux bateaux de décharger leur cargaison. Un grand port a des quais en pierre et en ciment. L'eau y est profonde. Les cargos et les paquebots peuvent y accoster.

Photo M. Renaudeau/Hoa-Qui.

Fig. 1 - Un avion d'Air-Afrique vient de se poser.
Il a roulé sur les pistes et s'est immobilisé... Les voyageurs descendent.

OBSERVONS

Autour de nous : Des avions se posent-ils près de notre village ? Où ? Y viennent-ils régulièrement ? Avons-nous vu un avion ? Combien a-t-il de réacteurs ou d'hélices ? Que transporte-t-il ?

Les documents : La *figure 1* nous montre un avion qui vient d'atterrir. Montrons un réacteur, les hublots.
La *figure 2* représente un aéroport au Congo. Que voyons-nous ? Comment sont faites les pistes d'atterrissage ? Qu'attendent les avions ?

LEÇON

Ali est allé à l'**aéroport** de **Yoff,** à côté de Dakar. L'**aéroport** est une sorte de grande gare où arrivent et d'où partent les **avions.** Il a vu un beau **bâtiment** où les passagers attendent, et des hangars où on vérifie les avions.

Il a vu les grandes **pistes** cimentées qui servent au **décollage** et à l'**atterrissage** des avions. Il a vu la **tour de contrôle** depuis laquelle sont dirigés tous les avions. Au bout de la grande piste, Ali a vu un gros avion qui se préparait à partir. A côté de ce gros appareil d'**Air Afrique,** les hommes paraissent bien petits.

Le **pilote** fait rugir ses **réacteurs.** Ils

Photo C.I.M.

Fig. 2 - L'aéroport de Brazzaville (Congo)
Sur les pistes, les avions attendent le moment du départ.

sifflent de plus en plus fort. L'avion roule sur la piste, puis **décolle** et s'élève dans le ciel. Il emporte vers **Niamey** plus de deux cents passagers, leurs bagages et du courrier.

Cet avion vole très vite. Il fait près de 1 000 km à l'heure. Dans moins de quatre heures, il atterrira à Niamey.
Tous les jours, de nombreux avions atterrissent à Yoff et en décollent. Ils relient Dakar à tous les pays d'Afrique et à de nombreux autres pays du monde.

Dans l'avion, les voyageurs sont installés dans des fauteuils très confortables où ils peuvent se reposer ou lire. L'hôtesse apporte les repas ou des boissons rafraîchissantes. Quelques voyageurs dorment dans leur fauteuil.

QUESTIONS ET EXERCICES

Avons-nous vu un avion de près ? Combien avait-il de moteurs ou de réacteurs ?
Cherchons des gravures d'avions.

Y a-t-il un aéroport dans notre région ? Lequel ? Combien d'avions y atterrissent chaque jour ? D'où viennent-ils ? Vers où repartent-ils ?

Avez-vous reçu des lettres par avion ? D'où ? Combien de jours ont-elles mis à vous parvenir ?

RÉSUMÉ

A l'aéroport de Yoff, Ali a assisté au départ d'un avion d'Air Afrique. L'avion, poussé par 4 réacteurs, roule sur la piste cimentée puis décolle. Il emporte plus de 200 passagers, leurs bagages et du courrier et relie, entre elles, les grandes villes africaines.

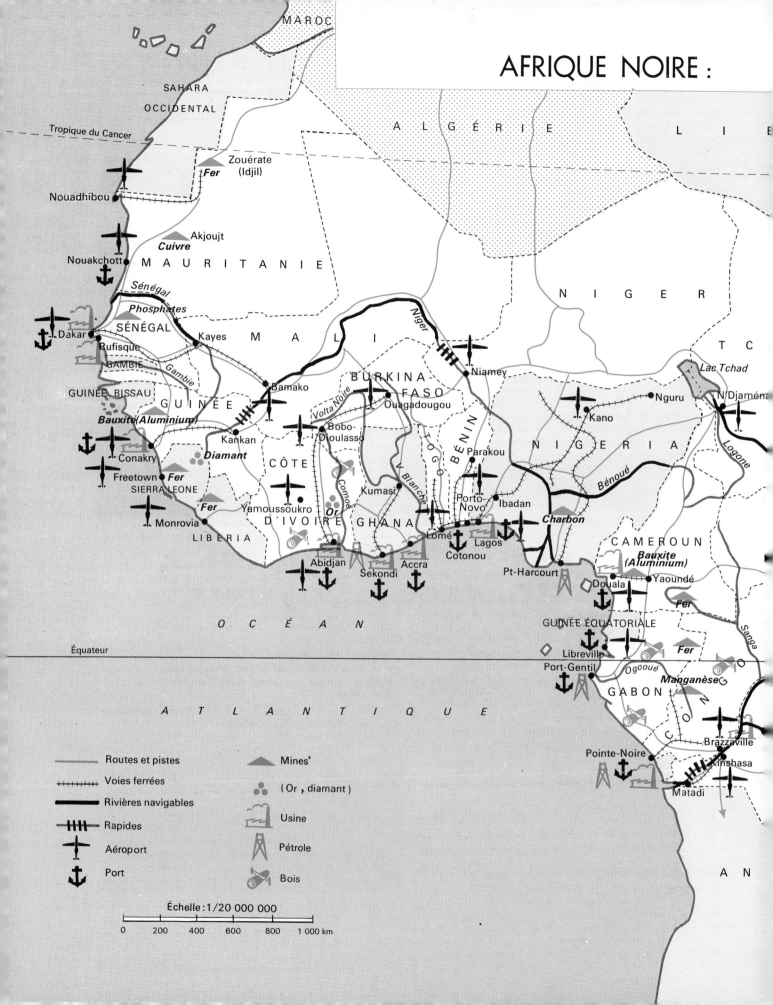

AFRIQUE NOIRE:

MAROC

SAHARA
OCCIDENTAL

Tropique du Cancer

ALGÉRIE   LI

Fer Zouérate
(Idjil)

Nouadhibou

Akjoujt
Cuivre

Nouakchott

M A U R I T A N I E

N I G E R

Sénégal

TC

Phosphates

SÉNÉGAL   Kayes   M A L I

Dakar

Niger

Lac Tchad

Rufisque

Niamey   N Djaména

GAMBIE   Gambie   Bamako

BURKINA
FASO

Nguru

GUINÉE BISSAU   GUINÉE   Volta Noire   Ouagadougou

Kano

N I G E R I A

Logone

Bauxite(Aluminium)   Bobo-
Dioulasso   Parakou   Bénoué

Conakry   Kankan   **Diamant**   Kumasi   Porto-   Ibadan

Freetown   **Fer**   CÔTE   Comoë   **Or**   V.Blanche   Novo   **Charbon**

SIERRA LEONE   **Fer**   Yamoussoukro   GHANA   Lomé   Lagos   CAMEROUN

Monrovia   D'IVOIRE   Cotonou   Pt-Harcourt   **Bauxite
(Aluminium)**

LIBERIA   Abidjan   Sekondi   Accra   Douala   Yaoundé

Fer

GUINÉE ÉQUATORIALE

O C É A N   Libreville   **Fer**

Équateur   Port-Gentil   Ogooué   **Manganèse**

A T L A N T I Q U E   GABON   C   O   N   Brazzaville

Pointe-Noire   Kinshasa

Matadi

AN

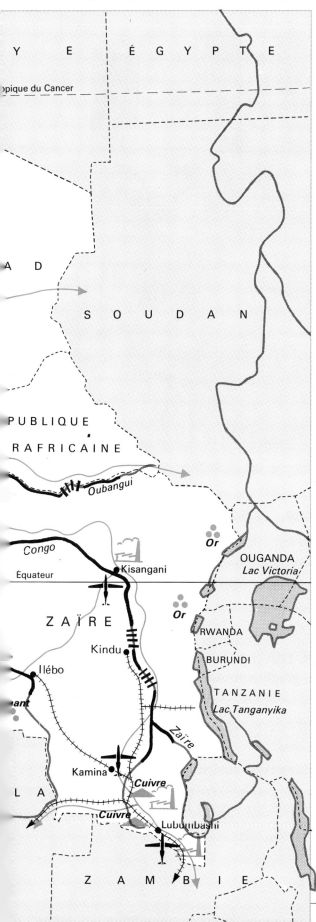

La carte nous montre les grandes voies de communication de l'Afrique Noire, les ports et les grandes villes où il y a des usines. Chercher ces villes sur la carte.

Que fabrique-t-on dans les usines?

La carte nous montre aussi les produits que l'on trouve dans le sous-sol de notre pays. Quels sont ces produits?

Les productions de nos cultures, de nos mines, de nos usines sont embarquées sur les bateaux qui accostent dans les ports de Nouakchott, Dakar, Conakry, Monrovia, Abidjan, Accra, Lomé, Cotonou, Lagos, Douala, Libreville, Pointe-Noire et Matadi.

De ces ports partent des chemins de fer. Jusqu'où conduisent-ils? Des routes relient entre elles les grandes villes de l'intérieur. Cherchons quelques-unes de ces routes qui partent de notre pays ou qui y arrivent.

Certains fleuves navigables portent des bateaux. Lesquels?

Citons les principaux aéroports de l'Afrique Noire,

QUESTIONS ET EXERCICES

Je veux me rendre d'Abidjan à Niamey. Quelles voies de communication puis-je emprunter?
Même question pour : Dakar-N'Djaména, Douala-Bangui, Matadi-Lubumbashi, Conakry-Abidjan.

43 VOYAGE AUTOUR DU MONDE

Photo Kammerman.

Fig. 1 - Paris : l'île de la Cité et la cathédrale Notre-Dame.

Photo M. Renaudeau/Hoa-Qui.

Fig. 2 - Un quartier de New York (Etats-Unis).

OBSERVONS

Autour de nous : Quels sont les bateaux ou les avions qui quittent notre pays ? D'où partent-ils ? Où vont-ils ? Y a-t-il, dans notre région, des hommes venant d'autres pays du monde ?

Les documents : Ils représentent des villes et des paysages photographiés dans les différentes parties du monde. Que voyons-nous de particulier sur les *figures 1, 2, 3 et 4* ? Connaissez-vous dans votre région un paysage semblable à celui de la *figure 4* ?

LEÇON

Le grand frère de Fatou a beaucoup voyagé. Il a quitté l'Afrique par avion pour l'**Europe**. Il a atterri à **Paris** qui est la capitale de la **France** *(figure 1)*.

L'**Europe** est le pays de l'homme blanc. Beaucoup d'Européens sont cultivateurs ou éleveurs. D'autres, très nombreux, travaillent dans de grandes usines.

De Paris, le frère de Fatou s'est envolé vers l'**Amérique**. Elle est peuplée de Blancs, de Noirs, anciens esclaves, et de quelques Peaux-Rouges.

Les cultivateurs américains ont d'immenses champs qu'ils cultivent avec des machines. L'Amérique possède d'immenses usines et

90

Fig. 3 - Un petit village japonais, au bord de la mer.

Fig. 4 - Paysans au travail dans une rizière, en Indonésie.

aussi de très grandes villes dont les immeubles sont si hauts qu'on les appelle des **gratte-ciel** *(figure 2)*.

New York est une des plus grandes villes du monde.

Poursuivant son tour du monde, le frère de Fatou arrive en **Extrême-Orient,** au pays des hommes jaunes, en **Chine,** au **Japon** *(figure 3),* au **Viêt-nam** et en **Indonésie** *(figure 4).* Le paysan asiatique est un adroit cultivateur. Sa petite rizière produit beaucoup de riz. Il mange du poisson et boit du thé.

Il vit dans de gros villages, mais l'Extrême-Orient a aussi des villes très peuplées.

Noir, blanc, rouge ou jaune, où qu'il soit, l'homme travaille.

QUESTIONS ET EXERCICES

Suivons, sur le planisphère ou, mieux, sur le globe terrestre, le voyage effectué par le frère de Fatou. Montrons l'Europe, l'Amérique, le pays des hommes jaunes.

Comment cultive-t-on le sol en Amérique ? Comment nomme-t-on les grands buildings de New York ?

Quelle est la principale production agricole des hommes jaunes ? Fait-on la même culture dans votre région ?

RÉSUMÉ

L'Europe se trouve dans la zone tempérée. L'Amérique a l'agriculture la plus riche, de très grandes usines et de très grandes villes. Les paysans d'Extrême-Orient sont de grands producteurs de riz.

44 LES ÉCHANGES DANS LE MONDE

Fig. 1 - Une caravane transporte des barres de sel dans le désert de Mauritanie.

OBSERVONS

Autour de nous : Allons au marché et notons ce que les commerçants y apportent et ce qu'ils achètent aux cultivateurs du village.

Les documents : La *figure 1* nous montre une caravane. De quels animaux est-elle constituée ? Où chemine-t-elle ? Que peut-elle transporter ?
La *figure 2* nous montre un grand port de commerce. Que voyons-nous sur les quais ? Par quels moyens les sacs sont-ils montés sur le bateau ?

LEÇON

Les paysans de notre village envoient au **marché** tout ce qu'ils produisent : le riz, le maïs, les bananes, des œufs, du beurre, des poulets, en un mot des produits alimentaires. Des **dioulas** achètent ces produits pour les revendre aux habitants des villes.

Le paysan achète, en échange, des tissus, des outils, des ustensiles de cuisine que le dioula a ramenés de la ville.

Les différents pays de l'Afrique Noire **échangent** entre eux de grandes quantités de produits. Mais les produits africains vont encore bien plus loin.

De grands bateaux portent dans le monde les

Fig. 2 - Embarquement des sacs d'arachide sur un cargo.

bois précieux de nos forêts, les bananes, les ananas, le café, le cacao, les palmistes de nos plantations, les arachides de nos champs, les minerais et le pétrole de notre sol.

En échange, ces pays nous envoient les **produits fabriqués** dans leurs usines :

des conserves, des tissus, des vêtements, des machines et des automobiles.

D'autres produits viennent de pays très éloignés. L'**Extrême-Orient** nous envoie ses automobiles, ses appareils de radio à transistors, ses téléviseurs ; l'**Amérique** nous envoie du blé, de la farine, des machines...
Tous ces échanges nous montrent combien, pour vivre, les hommes de tous les pays ont besoin les uns des autres.

QUESTIONS ET EXERCICES

Quels produits notre village envoie-t-il aux villes voisines ?
Quels produits notre région envoie-t-elle dans des pays au-delà de la mer ?

D'où viennent les marchandises que nous achetons au marché ou dans les boutiques de notre village ?
Quels produits nous arrivent d'Extrême-Orient ? d'Amérique ?

RÉSUMÉ
La campagne envoie à la ville des produits alimentaires et en reçoit des produits fabriqués qui viennent souvent de pays lointains. L'Afrique expédie dans le monde le bois, les bananes, le café, les arachides, le pétrole et les minerais. Elle en reçoit des tissus, des automobiles, des machines et bien d'autres produits fabriqués dans le monde entier.

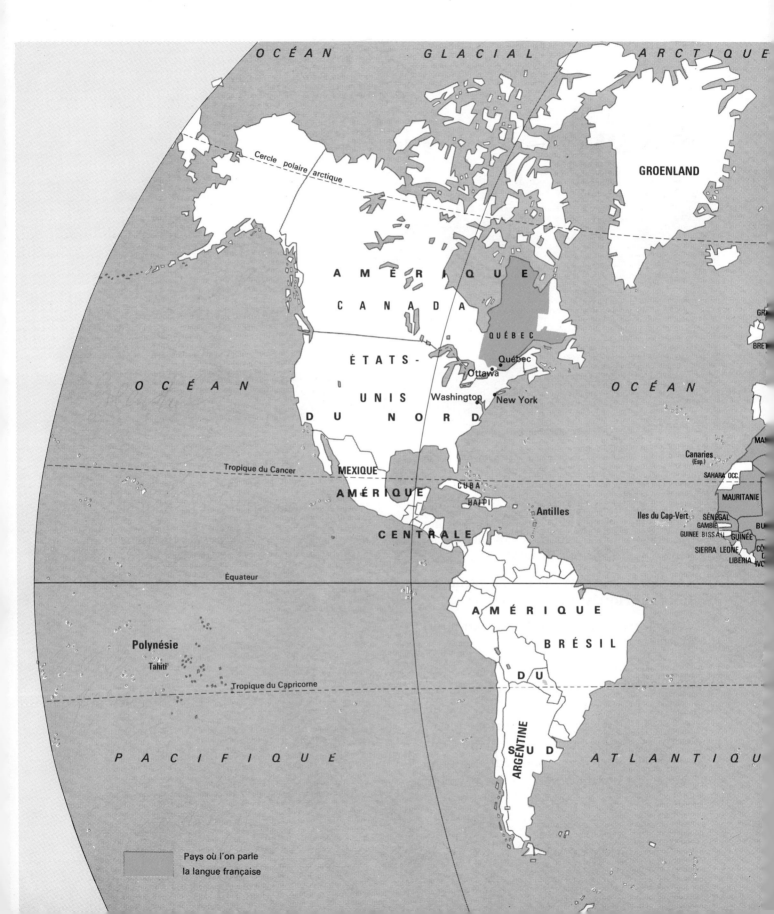

OCÉAN GLACIAL ARCTIQUE

GROENLAND

Cercle polaire arctique

AMÉRIQUE

CANADA

QUÉBEC

Québec

ÉTATS-

Ottawa

UNIS

Washington • New York

DU NORD

OCÉAN

OCÉAN

GR

BRE

MA

Canaries
(Esp.)

Tropique du Cancer

MEXIQUE

SAHARA OCC.

CUBA

AMÉRIQUE

MAURITANIE

HAÏTI

Antilles

Iles du Cap-Vert

SÉNÉGAL

CENTRALE

GAMBIE

BU

GUINÉE BISSAU

GUINÉE

CÔ

SIERRA LEONE

D

LIBÉRIA

IVC

Équateur

AMÉRIQUE

BRÉSIL

Polynésie

DU

Tahiti

Tropique du Capricorne

SUD

ARGENTINE

PACIFIQUE

ATLANTIQU

Pays où l'on parle
la langue française

The Nightmare Solution

The Nightmare Solution

Simple, Creative Methods for Working Out Your Dream Problems

With Guidance for Parents, Therapists, and Teachers Helping Children

Ann Sayre Wiseman

ECHO POINT BOOKS & MEDIA, LLC

Published by Echo Point Books & Media,
www.EchoPointBooks.com

ISBN: 978-1-62654-979-1

Cover artwork © 1929 *Strong Dream*, Paul Klee

Cover design by Adrienne Nunez,
Echo Point Books & Media

Printed in the U.S.A.

For all children everywhere,
and for the child in each of us.

ACKNOWLEDGMENTS

First, my thanks go to the children whose dreams and drawings illustrate this book. They know who they are, even though I have changed their names to protect their privacy. My thanks to the three women who made this book possible by welcoming the pilot workshops at their schools: Betty Buck, former headmistress of Milton Academy Lower School; Virginia Kahn, director of the Atrium School; and Linda Brown (and her teachers) at Fayerweather School.

Thanks to my two typists, Sylvia DeMurias and Carmeline, who transcribed the tapes; to my son, Kiko, who edited the first edition; to Bob and Holy Doyle for the generous use of their laser printer; Jakie Wan for help in smartening up the second edition, and to Mrs. George Young for putting in the good word that clinched the initial publication of the second edition.

FOREWORD

The helpful tools offered here are as basic as A-B-C and, like the alphabet, just as easy and powerful! The woman who developed them was an artist and art therapist who kept sketch journals through a long life of travel, work, family, and investigation, including many years of pioneering work in the field of expressive therapy. So when she was faced with a classroom of graduate students all hoping to sort out and solve complex problems and issues, she did what came naturally and said: "show me a picture, make me an image, draw me a map."

Her goal, however, was not to make artists out of dreamers, but to help dreamers make sense of their own images, experiences, and stories. So she asked the questions you ask when you see a picture: "What does it mean? Why those colors? How does it make you/me/us feel?" Her questions and encouragement gave her students faith in their birthright of language: the manipulation of symbols—objects, drawings, images—to create and convey meaning. We all have a story, and our job in life is to give it meaning and share it.

We don't know how much of the dreaming mind is individual, and how much of it might come from a "collective unconscious," but dreams invite each one of us to participate in a fascinating project of exploration and discovery. The method in this book makes it easy and fun to draw important and useful connections between your life, your feelings, and the images created by your dreaming mind.

"A picture is worth a thousand words."

An old cliché, but true: we build our lives—all our systems of communication, language, and culture—on a foundation of images. True, we need words to explain and share them, but it all begins with images—and feelings.

To make sense of images, we put them into context, and make them into a story, for only in that kind of context can we draw out their meaning.

The challenge and delight of understanding dream images—even scary ones—is discovering how we feel about what's happening in our life, and what we can do about it. This book will help you do that, even if you're afraid. Ultimately, it is a way toward problem solving for any challenge at all. I hope you enjoy the adventure.

—Kiko Denzer, author, artist, publisher, and father

PS:

Ann Sayre Wiseman passed away in April of 2013 at the age of 86; she wrote 13 other books celebrating art and human creativity; she was also my mother. My brother and I grew up watching (and, when we could, helping) her as she earned our living as an artist and single-mom, managed house and family, traveled, and pursued her own continuing education. She showed us how to live a free, interesting, and creative life with whatever materials were given.

She believed in creative potential, absolutely—given innate human imagination and will, there was no situation to which creative force couldn't be applied; no problem of living couldn't be at least creatively addressed. This kind of thought-in-action solves problems, wards off despair, empowers love and curiosity and hope—it offers powerful medicine for facing your own nightmares, someone else's, or life's daytime problems.

I didn't realize what a gift it was until I was in my thirties, and decided to make a life of my own instead of pursuing a salary, status, or job-title. As I set about pursuing my dreams, I came to appreciate all the tools I'd learned from watching and helping my mother at work.

Whether or not you already have such tools, this book offers opportunities to practice their use in creative, helpful ways—I'm delighted to be able to help make it available for another generation of parents, children, and teachers.

Publisher's PPS:

To give context to the words above, it seems worth telling you a bit about Kiko. Before we met (online and via a number of phone calls), I was aware of Kiko as an author and publisher. His best known and much in demand book, *Build Your Own Earth Oven,* is considered one of, if not *the*, definitive book on the topic. As a bookseller, I've heard dozens of spontaneous testimonial/reviews about how great his book is. In addition to being practical, *Build Your Own Earth Oven* has heart and integrity—which, after getting to know Kiko a little bit, makes sense; he is warm, kind, and thoughtful. He is also a carpenter/builder, community developer, editor, and musician. In others words, he lives a full and creative life. I mention this because sometimes you hear about authors who don't eat their own cooking. In the case of Ann Wiseman and her son Kiko, who has adopted her creative methods, the proof is in the proverbial pudding—and it's a nutritious one. So I invite you to dig in too!

—Marshall Glickman, publisher Echo Point Books & Media

Contents

The Nightmare Solution

Introduction

This book is about an approach to solving dream problems which I developed over the past fifteen years while working with large groups of adult graduate students training in the expressive therapies at Lesley College in Cambridge, Massachusetts. Using this technique, I could handle eighteen to twenty students at a time and keep them all busy working out their own dream problems. I call this process "mapping a problem on the paper-stage."

I have simply borrowed from Gestalt psychology, psychosynthesis, and psychodrama and created a modified mini-system for working with dreams which I call auto-drama. The idea of confronting the enemy and finding the gift in the dream is from the work of the anthropologist Kilton Stewart and the Indians from whom he took many of his ideas.

SETTING UP THE PAPER-STAGE

It is sometimes tedious to listen to the endless details of a person's dream that are so important to the dreamer, but not to the guide. Partly in self-defense against tedium and to make the program more interesting and concrete, I ask my students not to tell their stories but to show me what the problem looks like. They lay their story out on a sheet of paper so guide and participant can understand it visually, as observers. The dream details are turned into colored paper symbols which can be invested with the proper characteristics, attitudes, and emotions. Color, size, and shape play an important part. Color is a language in itself, giving the guide, as well as

the dreamer, a great deal of rich, gratuitous information. Affinities between members of a family usually take weeks to explain verbally, while on the paper-stage, they are immediately visible. We get more information in fifteen minutes from this method than you get in ten talk sessions. This saves time and gets right to the issue.

The figures can be flat or three dimensional, torn symbols or figurative. No skill is needed. No one need feel artistically inhibited. We bypass the fact that adults, in general, are not comfortable when asked to draw or act.

I found it very practical to reduce the visual stage to a mere piece of paper. In this way, everyone in a group can work at once in their own private arena. Each participant using the paper-stage can encompass and govern the entire scenario themselves. They are the observer as well as director and self-therapist. They can work through a dream with or without a guide, performing the auto-drama, reversing roles with the dream characters, dialoguing, and testing options, checking out their feelings, while protecting their own integrity. This process is free of the clumsy interference of other live bodies and, since the dreamer plays all the parts and harvests their own projections, the resolution can move quite fast. The dreamer does all the work because our projections are the limitation of our understanding.

Since I believe we each have our own answers, it is just a question of how to get at them. The paper-stage approach feels exactly right for this work and uses a lot of the good tools from many practices.

To get started, I use a series of provocative questions that each participant can relate to in their own way. Questions like: What do you like and dislike about this scene? What needs to happen to make it feel right for you? What options are available to you? If change is in order, what is the price of change? What is the problem doing for you? The ultimate goal is to move the dreamer towards a satisfactory resolution of the dream problem.

This method not only allows the leader to guide many people at the same time, but it empowers the dreamer by putting them in charge. No one has to wait; all can start to explore their options immediately. Later, when all the basic work is done, we can go more deeply into one person's issues while the group listens and piggybacks on the questions, thereby learning the process.

ADAPTING THE PAPER-STAGE FOR WORK WITH CHILDREN

This is a wonderfully simple, straightforward approach, and is very useful. I decided to modify this method in order to try it with children, and asked some school groups to help me put it into their language.

Several private schools were interested in a pilot program, and over the course of two winters, we invited about 300 children, ages five through thirteen, to attend my workshops. I decided to focus on nightmares to begin with because of the emergency factor. I used the same basic approach as I do with adults, except that, because children are natural, spontaneous artists, it was clear they preferred to draw their dreams onto the paper-stage. Then we would ask the dream images in the picture to speak for themselves. The dialogue is also spontaneous because everything in the dream can freely express its point of view.

First we make the dreamer feel safe enough to reenter a scary dream, and then we explore some alternative solutions. The results were so satisfying and empowering that the children also brought in their school problems to solve as well as their nightmares. These rehearsals helped them experience the cause and effect of their actions and beliefs.

We'd hit upon a visual method for negotiating resolution, a method so simple it requires no specialized training or equipment. You do not need a degree in child psychiatry or dream therapy—just paper, colored pens, patience, an open mind, and a sympathetic ear. With a group of children on the beach we

used shells, pebbles, and sticks with every bit as much success. This is nothing more than what my brothers did with knives, forks, and peas on the kitchen table to explain a play in baseball. These are other ways of setting up the paper-stage.

It is not dream analysis, nor is it a form of psychoanalysis. The aim is not to analyze the child, the dream, or the imagery, but rather to approach the dream story as a problem to be solved in a way the dreamer finds useful so they learn more about themselves. The aim is to alter behavior that keeps us stuck. The focus is on the literal content of the dream. Discussion inevitably reveals the metaphoric message, the hidden or disguised meanings, but it is not necessary or even desirable to dwell on them. The manifest content in a dream is material enough to start with.

One of the benefits of this process is that it teaches negotiation skills. Nightmare sufferers are often found in a victimized position and usually need "permission" to defend themselves. The picture helps the child step outside of the victim situation and become the negotiator, the helper, and the problem solver. Making the dream visible helps remove the child from the immediate danger. (One tricks oneself into a position of power by asking, "What can I do to help that other self?")

During these workshops, the dialogues were taped and transcribed, and the drawings were Xeroxed. From this collection I have selected a sampling that deals with common concerns of children. I've included several drawings by adults because they were recurring childhood dreams, and some of the more complex dialogues that will show you how some dreamers were guided to their solutions.

I have chosen these resolutions and pictures to share with you the ingenious solutions and styles of empowerment the children have created. Since we all learn from the experience and example of others, seeing what worked may help you and your children take courage to jump in and begin.

WHAT ARE DREAMS?

No one knows for sure what dreams are or why dreams come, but I believe that everything the body does has a purpose and a good use. I can always find a gift in the dream. Some dreams give us problems, some give us affirmations, some are rehearsals or preparations for things to come. They often bring us warnings and let us know how we feel when we don't seem to know the extent of our feelings. The images a dream brings us are a more exact description of our feelings than words can express, especially regarding the complex nuances of feelings. Sometimes a dream appears as a *koan*, a Zen teaching story—a paradoxical riddle or conundrum which can only be solved irrationally. We work on it for years until one day we are able to reframe it so it makes sense.

Dreams and nightmares can be seen as metaphoric messages alerting us to problem areas in our life. Dreams come disguised in order to protect us. The Sufis teach through parables, as have many other cultures, in order to deliver a lesson indirectly. That, I believe, is also the way of the dream.

I believe too, that if we have received a dream we are ripe to deal with it. Dreams are like messengers alerting us to imbalance, telling us something is out of synch, forcing us to risk, stretch our limits, or back off and wait. (If hidden meanings are not ripe don't push it. Wait for the next dream.)

Dreams can present us with a paradox that bewilders us or wisdom that amazes us. We wonder how we know such things, wisdom greater than our own. We must be a kind of conduit to the higher beings, at times, through which revelation passes. Help your children respect their dreams and dreams will become a lifelong friend and guide. Keep a dream journal, even if you don't always have time to work on them. The accumulated stories and images will reveal their own sense in time.

I call this approach to dream-work *satisfying the image*. The idea came to me in a dream. I saw myself standing on the rim of the universe listening to a giant megaphone in the sky out of which shouted these words: "The solution is in the Image. FIND THE IMAGE AND SATISFY IT!" I knew immediately that was a key to problem solving, the key to dream-work.

When the dream image is seen as a metaphor, it acts like a picture describing feelings and the inside point of view. I think of this as the body's voice indicating trouble areas. In psychotherapeutic techniques, such as Transactional Analysis, Gestalt psychology, psychosynthesis, and psychodrama, the image is always the key. This process never fails to illuminate, and restaging a problem visually provides a wealth of additional information that surpasses words. "A picture is worth a thousand words," and dreams are the picture language.

GETTING UNSTUCK

The idea and practice of reentering a dream, listening, acknowledging, repairing old traumas, and creating a resolution has been most helpful in dealing with unfinished business and unresolved material. This mode of creative resolution has also been the fastest, most satisfying way to unblock stuckness.

Kilton Stewart, the anthropologist who introduced the idea of the Senoi dream culture into the study of dreams, told this story to a friend of mine. He described an incident that occurred when he was a boy of nine and accompanied his Mormon father on a trip into Utah Indian country. His father was surveying land there with a group of Harvard students. One night young Kilton wet his bed and was too embarrassed to leave his bunk in the morning, so he pretended to be sick. An Indian who wanted to trade his bow for young Kilton's knife came and asked for the boy. The cook said he was in bed sick. "What did you dream last night?" the Indian asked the boy. The boy replied, "I was sitting on the floor by my mother at her sewing machine. A little fox stuck his head around the door. I tried to alert my mother who didn't pay attention. The little fox came over and tickled me on my stomach which confused me and made me laugh and wet myself. That woke me up." He said this was a recurring dream, and every time he had the dream, he wet his bed. The Indian told him that the fox was a good sign and that he would be guided by fox wisdom, so he needn't feel upset or wet his bed anymore. And he never did.

This childhood incident may have been seminal to the work Stewart did as an adult. He spent much time studying and writing about the Senoi tribe of Malaysia. He was particularly interested in their mode of handling dreams, and became known for his dream theories. My friend believes he created his Senoi dream approach out of a melange of ideas he took from American Indians, the Senoi tribe, and from the Mormons. (Brigham Young believed in dreams, and founded the Mormon religion after receiving a dream message that sent him West.) She says Stewart did dream counseling on Park Avenue in New York City, and his confront-and-resolve approach to dreams was very popular. We develop the thing that works, whether or not it can be verified.

We used this method on our son, Piet, long before I became a dream-worker. When Piet was very young, he had bad dreams about the house burning down. My husband had heard of Stewart's approach and suggested Piet re-dream the dream and put the fire out. Next time he dreamed that dream, he came down at breakfast full of excitement to tell us he'd put the fire out. We asked him how, and he said, "I peed on it!"

Part of the power is in the permission to confront and resolve. Stewart's Senoi approach caught on as interest in dreams exploded some years ago, and it works. I have modified the need to kill the enemy because that no longer works.

Common sense will be your best guide in using this book. The first section explains the basic process and gives the rationale behind it. Children can read the children's section alone or with an adult or just get ideas from looking at the pictures of the dreams and their solutions in the section called "Nightmares and Their Solutions." The verbatim dialogues that led to the solutions will show you how to follow the dreamers lead, how to stop at obstacles, and how to respect fear, explore alternative routes, and hang in there until the child finds a way out.

I have great faith in the sophistication and wisdom of children, and their knowledge of what is right for them. Children have their own answers according to their own readiness if you will give them a chance to guide you.

In rereading these dialogues I recognize how I have often used leading questions indicating that I had my own idea where things should go. I will leave them in so you can see we are only human and maybe you can remember to check yourself by feeling critical of me.

I offer you this book with thanks to the children who taught me to have tremendous respect for their innate honesty, intelligence, and creative originality. And to emphasize that children, new as they are to this life, do possess the knowledge of what's right for them, and given permission to trust themselves, given their own organic timing and a sympathetic helper to explore their problems, will find their own best answers.

PART I
Adults' Section

DREAMS AND NIGHTMARES

No one knows for certain what dreams are, or why we dream, but we do know that we all have them every night even if we can't remember them. I like to think of the dream as a balancing voice, a message-giver from the interior self, an ally, and a gift. Dreams come to tell us something about ourselves, and offer us an opportunity to grow.

The dream is a unique resource for originality. For most people, it is a revelation to accept the idea that we are the creator of the dream. We are slow to own such creative power, such diabolical wit! But after working on a dream, we can delight in this innate ability, dare to listen to this metaphoric teacher-observer, and take charge of a new dimension of our own potential. After all, we are all simply conduits through which all psychic information passes, if only we learn how to open to it.

The dream can be seen as a challenge for the imagination of the day mind to match wits with the imagination of the night mind.

Often the dream appears as a metaphor which disguises our own identity or the focus of our anger, fears, or desires. When the dream comes to us in a voice so strong that it cannot be ignored, we call it a nightmare. Like a shout for help, it demands our attention. The dream messenger is telling us something is out of balance, or it forces us to look at feelings we dare not acknowledge in our waking life. Sometimes nightmares feel like it is a question of life or death. We need to take the time to process the feelings that are being described by this kind of dream. If we don't, the dream will just grow louder and nastier, and keep recurring, and we will find ourselves waking in the middle of the night, crying for help.

BURIED TRAUMAS AND UNFINISHED BUSINESS

Buried feelings, like truth, sooner or later, will find their way out. Eventually these concerns demand acknowledgment or resolution and solace. Some of us are not content until we have told our secrets and woes on national television. Declaration and confessionals have been a solace for centuries in most religions. For others, this unfinished business surfaces in our dreams. Unfinished business keeps us stuck, keeps things from getting comfortably stored or filed away, which is why recurring dreams are so common.

Surely it is better that we find a way to use dreams for our own good than leave them unattended. One way of dealing with a troublesome dream is to look at it as a life position statement and ask "What do I like and what don't I like about this position"? To recognize one's position and explore changes, that is the gift.

Dreams are the artist at work in the night.

THE PROCESS

The next time your child is awakened by a bad dream, give support and comfort as you usually do, with hugs and reassurance, and when some measure of calm has been restored, instead of taking the usual it-was-only-a-dream-there-aren't-any-monsters approach, try acknowledging the monster. Tell your child to ask the monster not to come any more tonight because everyone needs some sleep. Say you'll talk about it in the morning—you'll even invite the monster to draw itself to prove how scary it is. Together you will look at it and find out more about this kind of fear.

The image language of dreams is richer and more colorful than the spoken language, more exquisitely concise and explicit than words. All we have to do is learn how to translate this picture language back into feelings. That's why we ask children to draw their dreams and let the picture speak.

When you harvest the feelings from the images, you have a life position statement in picture form. You almost always have an issue, a predicament or problem waiting to be acknowledged or solved. Consider this the gift of the dream.

Drawing the dream puts the dreamer in charge, so we start by giving the child some paper and felt markers or crayons. I give them black felt markers for the drawing so we can Xerox them and so the monsters are firmly imprinted on the paper and can't fade away. We do this to get the terror out of the head and down on the paper where it can't move. On paper, the monster can't get you.

REENTERING THE DREAM

After the dream has been captured on paper, the next step is to ask if the child feels safe enough to reenter the dream. The child needs to reenter the dream in order to confront the enemy and negotiate with it.

If it's too scary, they can draw in helpers or alternatives that shift the victim into a power position. If the child does not feel safe enough to reenter the dream, help the child create protection: a shield, a cage, or a telephone may help.

The questions I might start with are:

- *How do you feel about drawing this scary nightmare?*
- *How will you make yourself feel safe enough to look at this monster again?*
- *If it's too scary, would it help to draw yourself outside the picture?*
- *Close your eyes and let the monster draw itself.*
- *Create some helpers to give you courage. Draw them in.*

A picture is worth a thousand words.

SELF-PROTECTION

Children are quick to think of ways to empower and protect the stuck self, such as:

drawing a shield

becoming invisible

capturing the monster in a cage or trap

cutting the monster down in size

getting help from an expert, a specialist, a guide

getting a ladder or parachute

creating an army of friends

Trust the child: children know what they can cope with. (In the Toilet Paper dream, Juliet was terrified by a roll of toilet paper that kept pulling her up. As her guide, it seemed logical at first, to cut or break the paper to free her, but Juliet found it was there for a reason, and her own solution was better. Although the paper controlled her, it also afforded her protection, which only she understood.)

DIALOGUING WITH THE MONSTER

Consider the thought that the enemy may have something to tell you about yourself and your life. Don't kill it, dialogue with it. Consider its point of view. Maybe it has something to teach you. Find out what power it has over you and what that power is doing for you. Ask the monster what it wants and why it came.

By talking to it and listening to its complaints, you can better understand its anger and rage. Try whatever will enable the child to talk to the enemy. Communicate by long distance.

After the images in the drawing have been given a chance to speak, and after the child has heard all the points of view, it is clearer what needs to happen to create a solution. The situation in the drawing can begin to move. Since all these voices are in some way a part of the dreamer, a settlement must be found that is fair to all of the internal participants. It is a challenge to find a way to live in peace with all the conflicting parts of one's self. (In the Ice Cream Shooting Machine dream, Everett came to understand that running away was part of the problem. When he dared to confront the machine, with the intention of hearing its point of view, the machine became quite reasonable. It was possible for both dreamer and monster to gain from the negotiation. The new factor was the on-and-off switch and the addition of the heart. The child agrees to stick around if the enemy will develop more heart, if orders are gentler and not made in anger.)

The child is given the chance to face a problem and by listening and saying the dialogue, to actually exercise role reversal, explore new behavior, develop new understanding, and practice the art of negotiation. A behavior rehearsal is as good as experience; it moves the feelings. That alone empowers and creates an awareness that is the beginning of change.

When the child communicates with the monster, the monster almost always becomes more human. By the time it is invited to say what it wants and why it feels like attacking, the dreamer may begin to recognize their own buried angers or complaints. The monster's anger is often a mirror of the dreamer's own rage, frustration, or fear, of the unacceptable emotions we must repress.

THE ART OF NEGOTIATION AND PERSUASION

The art of negotiation and the art of persuasion are skills we rarely teach at home or in school. Children are encouraged to see parents and other adults as absolute law givers, and sometimes as gods who know best. Isn't it time to teach our children the art of negotiation, rather than the power of force and killing? Technology has shrunk our planet so that one person's actions can have global consequences. The conditions that threaten our world today are full of nightmares. Our only hope is that all the peoples of the earth will learn to talk to one another before we destroy our common resources. We can begin within ourselves, by learning to negotiate a fair agreement between our wants and restraints, and among our mind, body, and spirit. Most of us are at war inside our own bodies, hating this or that part of ourselves, and battling issues of self-worth. Threats and force no longer work, nor do bribery and deprivation as they're apt to backfire. Let us start by learning to communicate and negotiate with our own conflicting inner voices.

Not all dreams can be approached from this pacifist standpoint, as you will see, nor are all children open to this avenue of approach. And adults who don't trust themselves probably won't be able to trust their children. Nevertheless, this is a good place to start and the art of negotiation is a good way to begin.

RECREATING THE DREAM

Recreating the dream allows the dreamer to reexperience it, this time free of terror, and in a calmer frame of mind. Changing just one thing is usually enough to get the child moving towards a self-empowering solution. Marjory, in "The Undelivered Cake," gave her younger self a stick and shield. This was all she needed to allow her to confront the Indians who had destroyed the cake in all her previous dreams. She was finally able to deliver the formerly undeliverable cake.

ALTERING TIME

In the paper-stage, it is possible to go back and forth in time at will. Ron, in "The Bike Race" dream, started the race over again, changing the circumstances so that his friend would not have to die to make things fair. Jack, in "The Christmas Tree Ornament" dream, created a time machine that took him back to two years old. Joan found that drowning didn't catch her father's attention, so she came to life and decided to swim.

HELPERS VS SUPERPOWERS

The child may call upon real or imaginary helpers that aid in finding the way to a solution, but I encourage reality and prefer specialists as helpers—lawyers, guides, counselors, judges, or firemen, etc. Employing superpowers may help for a while, but in the end they are less satisfying than a self-empowering solution. Superman could have demolished Cliff's Whispering Bubba Ball, but negotiating for more authority over his life forced him to accept more responsibility and gave him more self-respect.

Help can come from someone close, for instance, a favorite teacher or relative. Joanna, in "The Unacceptable Divorce" dream, is consoled when she draws in her grandmother and asks for advice, and her grandmother says, "Divorce is not the end of the world." Let the child supply the dialogue: they know what they need to hear better than you do.

KILLING THE MONSTER

Killing the monster may be the child's first instinct. Boys particularly love to spear and bloody the wretched creature. It is safe enough to vent that power on paper, but the idea that the monster may return twice as terrible the next night helps them consider alternatives to killing. Since monsters very often reflect negative parts of ourselves, if we kill them, we kill that part of ourselves. We will never get the dream's message if we kill, nor will we understand why the dream sent this kind of messenger. If we are to learn to live with our own inner violence, anger, and hurt

> Robert Louis Stevenson wrote in his memoirs that his childhood nightmares were so frightening, he used to tell himself stories to keep from going to sleep. Later in life, he drew many of his literary works from these stories and nightmares that, he said, came to him from "the little people."
>
> "When I was in need of money, the little people would bestir themselves and labour all night to set before me their treacherous tales as if on the lighted stage. . . . All I do is the sitting at the table and the mailing out of the manuscripts, and market the dreams. The little Brownies do the rest." The story of Dr. Jekyll and Mr. Hyde was one of those that came to him as a gift of his dreams.

feelings, let us start by befriending our monsters. Find out why they have so much power over us. (Our enemies always have the most to tell us about ourselves.) It also helps to consider the idea that the monster may offer a gift by coming into our dream.

HIDING AND SELF-SACRIFICE

Many kids try to escape the dream by hiding under the covers, or under the bed. We wake from nightmares the moment we are totally victimized, on the verge of being caught or killed. We jump out of our skins. It is as though the dream maker has sacrificed the dreamer's life, and this is, perhaps, the definition of a nightmare. As the guide, you can help stimulate more challenging and interesting possibilities than allowing the self to be sacrificed.

Giovani's Conversation with a Bear

After being introduced to this idea of confronting the nightmare monster, Giovani, a nine-year-old Bahamian boy, came to see me several days later and said he'd had a dream that a bear was chasing him. He gave me this drawing of the bear and said:

I was very frightened it was the same bear that came before. I ran as fast as I could. The bear roared and roared until I had a headache. When I got tired, he nearly caught me. He followed me everywhere. I turned and twisted to dodge him. I couldn't take it anymore. . . . Finally I had to stop. I felt desperate and thought I was going to die, so I woke up. Then I remembered what you said about drawing the dream and talking to the monster. Next time I went to sleep he came back and instead of running, I asked him why he was scaring me. He said he was just trying to get some attention. "Every time I go into someone's dream," he said, "they run away. . . . You are the first person who stood up to me. I have no one to talk to so I get very angry, now we are friends."

UNMASKING THE METAPHOR

When connections are made, like the robot that sounds like dad, what trouble might it make at home, you may ask. Unmasking the metaphor is fine when it's spontaneous, but when it's the guide's curiosity, it's best to leave it disguised as it appeared in the dream, and simply use it as an allegorical situation to be solved.

FINDING SOLUTIONS

Because most of us have had little success coping with our own nightmares, we often feel impotent when we try to help our children. *Not knowing* what to do is something we all fear. Not knowing is something most teachers and parents prefer to avoid or deny. I hope that this book will make you feel more comfortable in not knowing the answers. All you are called upon to do is to provide the tools, and join your children in the spirit of the explorer. Children will recognize the solutions that are right for them.

This approach to creative resolution requires the dreamers to help themselves and to take responsibility for what they know. It establishes that only they know the usable answers, the proper steps on the path to change, and the solutions to their own problems or protection for their limitations. Nightmare fears are calmed by the very act of seeking a solution equal to the nightmare.

The effort alone threatens and weakens the oppressor and energizes the helpless.

Answers have to come in a way that we can use them: children will recognize solutions that suit their readiness and their skills of the moment, and will reject those that don't.

Sometimes we must try a number of solutions. Cliff told me, as we worked through his Bubba Ball nightmare, that he had tried many solutions in previous dreams: he'd tried reasoning with the enemy, tried doctors, tried holding his breath. This time he felt that wings and a parachute would help, along with the courage to ask for a little more authority and responsibility.

OBSTACLES

The obstacles that children pose are very important to the success of this work. Obstacles must be seen as our best guide to the integrity of the solution. They represent the omissions and small details that the problem may be built on. Molly dreams she is inside her burning house but can't get out. She has three obstacles to overcome before she can accept a solution:

1. She can't leave the house without permission.

2. She can't cross the street alone.

3. The doorknob is too high to open the door.

This should warn the guide that there are certain things that come first:

1. Permission to think for herself in an emergency.

2. Permission to speak to strangers when her parents are not available, in order to cross the street.

3. Permission to trust herself to solve the doorknob problem and encouragement to risk the challenge.

Only then is her integrity satisfied enough to allow her to save her own life. Do not think this perverse or resistant. This is essential to her learning process. The omissions are probably the factors that caused the nightmare in the first place.

The solutions that are the most satisfying are the ones we can use in our waking life, but it is not something to force. If the child creates a fantastic solution, perhaps that is what they need for the time being. In any case, there is healing in symbolic resolution. The act of defining and repairing the dream issue on paper is equal, in essence, to planting the seed of change in the dreamer's reality. Once the seed is set, the idea grows by itself. If the feelings register it, change becomes a fact, even if it is only symbolic—just a drawing on paper or a torn symbol. Even though it is "only a dream," real feelings are moved.

HELP FROM THE INNER GUIDE

I tell children that they have an inner guide, a loving voice within them that has their own best interests at heart. When they need help, they can go to the loving place inside and listen. It helps to close your eyes. A seventy-two-year-old man at one of my talks tried this and opened his eyes in tears. "My mother was there. She held me for the first time since I was two, when she died. I thought I'd never see her again."

Animals are wonderful guides. A little boy I saw last summer said he played the fool in class to get people to laugh but no one liked him. When I asked him what the fool was doing for him, he said "The joker in me keeps me from feeling. That's what the grown-ups do in my family, that's how to get along." He said he gets the most attention when he acts crazy.

I asked him to close his eyes and invite the animal who has the most wisdom to come into his mind and help him figure out what to do about this. When he opened his eyes, he reported that the owl had come and told him, "It's hard to be smart. It's easy to act stupid".

FEARS

Fear is a reaction to danger or anticipated danger, and is part of the body's normal defense mechanism. The physiological reactions associated with fear are rapid heart beat, loss of breath, paralysis, or muscle tension as the body prepares for fight or flight, or finds itself unable to move. So when a child has a nightmare, you can assume it will take a little time just for the body to resume its normal functioning. Patience and comforting are the best help. This is not the time for punishment and threats or name calling. Don't forget, you were there once, too small to defend yourself, too insignificant to count in the world of powerful human law-making giants.

Fear is partly instinctive, but is largely a learned response. Fear tells the body it needs to protect itself from real, anticipated, or imaginary danger. It tells us something bad is happening or is about to happen, and that we should try to avoid it, or warn somebody, or stop. It tells us something is wrong or too frightening to bear.

Fear usually tells us that more information is necessary before we can act in an emergency situation or cope with a challenge. If we have more information, we can usually deal with fear better, particularly if the fear surrounds something new we are supposed to do or try. It is a good rule, then, to respect fear and honor it instead of pooh-poohing it or putting ourselves down for being cowards.

We should not tell our children they are scaredy cats if they can't jump over their fears or push beyond them. Instead, we should help them rehearse and practice before they have to risk the whole person. Consider fear simply as a good guide.

Nightmare fears can be difficult to deal with. Very young children may not even understand that they have dreamed, for them there is no distinction between a dream image and reality. They may be convinced that the dream images are quite real, and no amount of searching the bedroom will make them feel safe enough to go back to sleep. After all, what's going to prevent the boogeyman from coming back again? Lights usually help, as will the presence of an adult, but this book will open lots of new angles that relieve anxiety.

Older children can better differentiate between dream image and reality, but can be just as frightened by the power of the dream, their feeling of helplessness, and the emotional impact. We really do not know the full dimension of our capacity to feel. I believe dreams introduce us to new dimensions of feeling.

I am constantly amazed by the complexity and sophistication of the feelings expressed by children in their dreams. This should remind us that children are total PEOPLE in their own right, no matter how small and inarticulate. No matter how young, adaptable, and willing they are to dismiss their fears and feelings in order to please adults or keep their place in school and family.

We can all admit to fears, some of which last throughout our lives—fear of the dark, fear of abandonment, fear of attack, fear of punishment or pain, fear of loud noises, fear of drowning and suffocation, fear of animals. As adults, we are generally able to get over our fears, or at least put them aside, hide from them, or learn to live with them. But the fears of small children threaten their very existence, and can render them totally helpless because they are so dependent. As maturity and experience bring a better understanding of the environment and our powers and right to defend ourselves, some fears tend to diminish. On the other hand, the fears of older children can be quite complex and sophisticated, therefore more difficult to express and more difficult to deal with. In fact, they may be impossible to solve. What solution is there for a child whose parents abuse them? or whose parents are involved in a bitter divorce? Even children from the happiest family situations will inevitably be exposed, sooner or later, to the uglier aspects of life—to death, violence, racial injustice. Fear of global nuclear warfare is very common in older children. The least we can do is acknowledge the child's awareness and try to address these shortcomings through our schools and communities, and in the way we lead our own lives.

DARING TO DRAW THE SCARY THING

Sometimes children are so frightened by their nightmares that they cannot even dare to draw them. If a dream has that kind of impact, the only way to dislodge it from the mind is to talk about it. It may help to look at some of the dream pictures in this book. Other children's solutions to nightmares may give courage. It helps to know other people have nightmares, and to share your own.

GUIDING

If you are going to play the part of the guide, consider that you know nothing. Do not diminish fear, do not give answers or solutions. Rather ask for the dreamer to find their own answers; try several, see which option FEELS right. Help them find a solution that they can handle. You are simply a follower who asks very simple questions like: What do you suppose the monster wants? If you could talk to it, what would you say? What would he/she/it say? (Is it a he/she/or it? Don't assume it's a HE just because our language uses "he" for everything.) How will you get the frightened self feeling safe enough to protect itself?

You can commiserate, suggest new angles, and accompany the dream worker, but do not create the solution. Don't presume to understand the problem. Help the child find their own satisfaction. You need no special training or license. You do need patience and respect for the child's ability and integrity.

Children are literal and that is the best approach to take with them and their dreams. Avoid the hidden meanings unless they recognize and make the connection—don't dwell on them. Remember, you, the adult authority, are very likely part of the problem. By working with the child you can help them with authority issues and they can help you modify your power over them.

Good or bad, all adults are teachers and we all have our own biases, convictions, and mind-sets which we are apt to pass on to the next generation, whether they are right for someone else, wrong for this new age, true or false. But we can't let this deter us from trying to help our children. We can only hope to learn with and from them . . . and you will be amazed at what children can teach you if you are open to hearing from them.

When I am guiding, it helps me to call upon my higher wisdom, that transpersonal ego-free dimension, in order to gain an overview that is larger and fairer than my personal limitations, larger than my personal projections, wiser than the feelings and attitudes which I am apt to attribute to others without checking first. I try to let the spirit of wisdom speak through me so that I am not so much a teacher, but merely a vehicle for wisdom. It often turns me around, freeing me of the urge to rescue, retaliate, or control. It doesn't always work (my biases are evident in many of the solutions: I don't allow killing to remain the solution for long).

If the guide's intention is clean, it helps to empty oneself of the investment in change and resolution. Some people need to stay stuck a little longer. I ask the child to decide what to look at and what to do. As guide, I try to remember to steer the rudder where the child chooses to go. My goal is to encourage autonomy so the child learns to empower themselves at whatever level they can handle.

This work continually reminds me to ask rather than assume I know the answer for someone else. The impact of Thad's dream, "Trapped in the World," hit me so hard, I feared I'd met the child who spoke for all of us who sit with the lighted fuse of world destruction deep in our hearts. His picture illustrated the despair I feel when I let the nuclear threat rise up in me. As guide, though, it was not important for me to express my feelings or to project my own meanings on Thad's dream, and so I restricted myself to the routine questions. I asked him what he needed for the boy in this picture. He said, "I need a place to hide so I can think." Since he could handle that need, I continued to stick to my questions: "Where will you hide so you can think?" And he created a box, and explained that the confusion was only in a certain place, not worldwide as I had thought.

SOME USEFUL QUESTIONS FOR THE GUIDE TO ASK:

- *What will you do to help the self in the picture?*

- *How does that feel to be stuck?*

- *What could you suggest if you weren't so frightened?*

- *What if you stretched your imagination?*

- *How will you make it less scary?*

- *Close your eyes and see yourself getting help. What do you see?*

- *If it could speak what would it say? (Everything has a point of view.)*

- *How can you control the monster so you can talk to it.*

- *Ask what it wants from you.*

- *What is his/her/its point of view? Do you think it has a point ?*

- *Then what? . . . Then what? . . . Then what?*

- *If you can't control or tame something, where can you put it?*

- *What would you like to tell the enemy?*

- *If you had some power what would you suggest?*

- *If there was a fair solution what would it be?*

- *What would help?*

- *Call upon a specialist who knows about these things.*

- *See yourself getting help.*

- *See yourself finding a solution.*

Questions like this keep the child moving toward a solution. Any small change will dislodge the impact of terror a bit. The guide reinforces that the dreamer is in charge of the dream. The picture is visible proof, and you are validating it. Only the empowered self can give good advice to the stuck self in a way that the stuck self can use it.

Studying the dialogues that accompany many of the dream solutions will give you a good idea of the process involved in guiding, and of the type of questions that are most effective.

Tool Kit for Guides

1. The key to arriving at a solution is to respect Sequential Progression: that means the child's concept of what comes next.

2. Think of it like a game of pick-up sticks. Without disturbing the pile, what stick can you dislodge next?

3. Consider that the child knows better than you what they can do next.

4. The guide, with patience, willingly follows the child's sequential steps towards the solution, respecting obstacles.

5. Don't mistake detours and obstacles as resistance, simply assume you may be asking the wrong question or going in the wrong direction.

6. It is important to let the child take the lead, because your assumptions, if not wrong, will probably be off the mark.

7. Careful use of the dreamer's own language helps to keep your assumptions from interfering with the dreamer's progress.

8. A solution may pose more fear than the problem itself. Don't forget to check that out first.

9. Joining the dreamer wherever the imagery takes you establishes reverence and trust for the dreamer's authority and leadership. Only then can the dreamer afford to reveal the goals, the path to change, and the obstacles which block it.

10. Guiding simply helps the dreamer acknowledge what they already know, but don't realize that they know.

11. Nightmares are almost bound to stir up strong emotions in the child, and it is important for the guide to acknowledge these feelings. Just as a wound must be cleansed before it can heal, anger, hatred, grief, and frustration need expression before forgiveness and spiritual healing can occur.

12. Work with the literal level of the dream, simply using the imagery provided by the dream without disturbing the hidden roots under the symbolic analogies. These are often too complicated and personal to look at directly, which may be why they come in disguise in the first place.

13. Respect the facts and don't argue with the reasons. (It was not necessary for me to know why Molly found the doorknob too high to reach, or if Everett's mother is like the ice cream shooting machine.)

WHEN WE ARE A PART OF THE PROBLEM

A certain amount of strain is built into every parent-child relationship. Many of the comments that follow the dream solutions in the second half of this book touch upon problems that commonly arise. Some parents create undo stress in their children's lives—usually without intending to and without realizing it. Consider that you, the parent, care-taker, or teacher may be part of the child's problem, so that it may be difficult for the child to work through a dream with you. Don't press it. Let it go. Give them encouragement to work it through alone or with someone else. Children are often so locked into fidelity, they cannot betray their negative feelings about their parents for fear of rejection. (One of my greatest pains as a child

was when my doting mother turned her back and left the room in disappointment at something I had done. I was totally controlled by that [harmless] gesture. It was perhaps more devastating than being whipped. Who knows?)

WHOSE FEELINGS ARE WE FEELING?

Close bonds with parents often make it difficult for a child to tell whose feelings they are feeling. Empathy can be confusing: when parents are afraid for their children, not only does it add to the child's fears, it interferes with the child's ability to risk new things on their own, or feel pleasure in a new situation if their parents fear it. The only way I can see to help with this is to urge parents not to make a child too special and not to live through them. If you are pressing the child to grow or change or shine, turn that focus upon yourself. Change yourself, shine yourself, become the thing you want someone else to be for you. It seems that people who force their kids to realize their dreams end up paying for it. The kid moves halfway round the world or goes into a totally different field

just to preserve their own identity. There is little help for overly-bonded children until they are out of their home. (Beware. If you're using dream-work to delve even deeper into the delicate channels of the over-bonded child, you will soon lose their trust. Better find them some outside help. Children can do this work together and get relief from their peers.)

JOKES, MOCKERY, AND SARCASM

Jokes at the child's expense create painful embarrassment. Mockery and sarcasm are two of the hardest things for children to deal with. (It took Judy twenty-eight years to forgive her father for his sarcasm and mockery in the dream "It's No Joke.") In the small classroom group setting or sitting around the kitchen table with family, it is important to create a safe reception of the delicate matter of dreams, so children can relate their dreams without risking ridicule.

PART II

Children's Section

LOCK YOUR MONSTER IN A CAGE

USE THE SAME WONDERFUL IMAGINATION THAT CREATED THE MONSTER

IF THIS BOOK IS YOURS PLEASE COLOR THE PICTURES

HELP IS HERE

Stop, look, and listen. . . .
You may learn something important.

Draw the dream.
Cage the monster.
Add your helpers:

Gods, gurus, grandmothers,
lawyers, teacher, specialists,
aunts, parents, friends,
police guards, guides,
fairy queens, godmothers,
monster-catchers with nets,
scientists with expertise,
seeing-eye dogs.

Let the picture speak.
Direct the rescue action.
Create a good solution.

Just draw help into your picture.
Invent a safe place.

Help is Here

WHAT ARE DREAMS?

Dreams give you a safe way to let off steam. Dreams are very useful, especially if you don't run away from them. Dreams can be helpers—and if you dare to look at them, they will teach you about yourself. Without your dreams, you might not recognize your feelings.

Nightmares are bad dreams. They are a safe way to experience bad things. Nightmares also introduce you to some strong feelings. They may tell you that you feel scared, alone, helpless, weak, frightened, left out. Sometimes these are new feelings, feelings so big they make you tremble, scream, fall out of bed, or cry for HELP.

Nightmares are designed to wake you up. Nightmares make you really SIT UP and LISTEN.

In this book, you will meet children like yourself who, at first, were very confused and frightened by their dreams, but after drawing pictures of the dreams and letting the dreams speak, the children created ways to give themselves more power over their dreams. You may get some new ideas from these pictures of how to control or befriend your scary monsters and empower yourself so you don't feel so frightened. You and your dreams can become friends.

The children who lent me the nightmares and drawings that appear in this book came to my dream workshop. First they drew the nightmare on paper so the monsters and bad things couldn't move. Then they thought of a way to make themselves feel safe enough to ask the picture to talk to them. Some children locked their monsters in cages. Some spoke to them by telephone. Some drew in helpers.

You will find many ways to stand up to monsters and get them to tell you why they came into your dream. You'll see new ideas for how to defend yourself and your feelings. You'll learn to negotiate (make a bargain) with the things in your nightmare that scare you.

It helps to talk about nightmares with someone who understands. The people in this book will help you see that you are not alone. Everyone has nightmares sometime in their life.

It's no fun carrying awful nightmares around in your head all day. It's even worse to be afraid to go to sleep for fear that you will dream bad dreams—so join our dream group and let these ideas help you.

being fired
flying
falling
being chased
being naked in public
tidal waves
losing teeth
houses and cars
being caught
being stuck
failing exams
being dead
being a baby
being robbed
being smothered
being held up
climbing ladders

STOP thief

police

Animals dream. Haven't you seen them running in their sleep, whimpering and shaking?

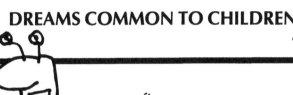

fire
falling
flying
giants
spiders
robots
dinosaurs
monsters
spaceships
being chased
being stuck
being lost
scary animals
deep water
bed wetting
weird people
being caught

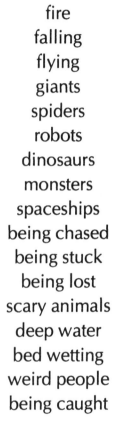

People big and small have similar feelings.

KILLING IS NOT A SOLUTION

Killing is common in dreams. So is violence. It is about the only place you can get away with it. We can do things in dreams that would put us in jail in waking life. Sometimes it feels great to kill the monster, or Hitler, or other bad things, but usually it bothers us and troubles our conscience.

Using this vein of thought, when you ask children if they think killing is the answer, they will rethink the problem. Usually they feel better about outsmarting the monster,

controlling it, restraining it, or negotiating with it. Killing scares us all because it is so final and heavy on the conscience. It is not comfortable for children to have full power.

Dreams of violence are usually telling us about our emotions . . . *that we feel angry enough to kill.*

In ancient times, killing would have made us heroes. Killing was thought to be brave and manly. But from now on, this planet is too fragile to use war and killing as a solution to anger or a means to settle problems and disagreements. We know now that war no longer works. No matter how far away the battles are fought or the bombs are dropped, the effects are so great they harm everyone wherever they are.

You who will be tomorrow's leaders need to learn new and better ways to keep peace, starting with listening to the arguments that go on inside yourself. Learn to exercise peacemaking skills in your body, starting with your nightmares.

Besides, the problem with killing dream monsters is that they often come back another night, even more terrible than before.

QUESTIONS TO ASK MYSELF

1. How do I feel when I look at this dream picture?

2. How can I make myself feel safe enough to reenter this scary dream?

3. If I use my imagination, can I create a solution that saves my life?

4. Is there a solution?

5. If I feel helpless, who can help me? Who can I talk to?

6. If no help is available, how can I help myself?

7. If this dream would upset my parents, can I create a *guide* to help me?

8. Is it fair for a dream monster to kill me?

9. If I have the right to save my life, can I do it in every nightmare? That's the challenge.

10. What are my strengths? When I feel bad about myself, it helps to name them.

11. What is the message in this dream? What is the gift in this dream?

QUESTIONS TO ASK THE MONSTER

1. Why have you come to scare me?

2. What do you want?

3. If I dare to stop running away, can we talk?

4. If monsters represent giant feelings, what feeling do you represent?

5. If you could talk, what would you say?

6. How would you feel if I scared you like this?

7. What's good about you?

8. I'll tell you what's good about me.

9. If we negotiate a deal, will you stop scaring me?

The intellect can only absorb what the emotions will allow.

Dr. Haim Ginott

WHAT ARE YOU DOING
IN MY DREAM?

Nightmares are like tigers loose in the mind
You can run and run and never escape,
You can wake up and fear to sleep,
Or you can stand still,
Confront the enemy, and ask
"What are you doing in my dream?"
Once the dream is down on paper
It cannot move.
You have the power to stop the action.
You can draw a cage around the bad thing.
You can create a net, a trap, a deep pit.
You can create a solution.
Consider a monster a picture of feelings,
Exaggerated, demanding to be heard,
Like fears that grow too big to hold inside.
What it's doing in your dream is getting your attention.
It's time to listen. . . . Don't run!
If your imagination can create the dream,
Your imagination will help you handle it.
You alone know the answer that feels right.
Stop screaming for help.
See what you can do to save yourself.

I CAN HELP MYSELF

I have imaginative solutions.

I'm learning to be independent.

I can learn to read picture language.

I can find someone to tell my nightmares to.

I can negotiate with everything in
my dream.

I can do it by myself if no one is
around to help.

I'm learning to know my feelings
and express them usefully.

I can get the bad thing out of my
head and on paper so the bad
thing can't move.

I have some good ideas and can try
them all until I find one I like.

I want to learn to negotiate instead
of running away.

I can draw my dream and step outside of it.

I have new ways of looking at
dreams.

I can confront the enemy in my
dream.

I can get to know myself better.

I can learn to make myself safe.

I can be in charge of the action.

I can learn to work with my dreams.

I'm learning to defend my feelings.

I have a healthy imagination.

I want to grow more daring.

I can comfort my fear.

I have permission to defend myself.

I am a wonderful human being.

I have the right to be alive and love
life.

PART III
Nightmares and Their Solutions

The sampling of dream problems in this section illustrates all the concepts that were covered in the adults' section of *Nightmare Help*. Each dream and its solution is described in the words of the dreamer, and each is followed by some brief comments that will call your attention to any significant details about the dreams, the methods used to arrive at their solution, or the problems the dream might represent. Some dreams are also followed by the dialogue between the guide and the child that will show you how different children allow a solution to come about. (The posing of obstacles usually means there are extenuating problems that must be addressed before the central issue can be resolved.) Finally, there are "discussion starters," questions that have been raised by children in my workshops. In going through the book with children, many questions are bound to arise. It is important to make room for this discussion if you are going to open these subjects in your home or at school.

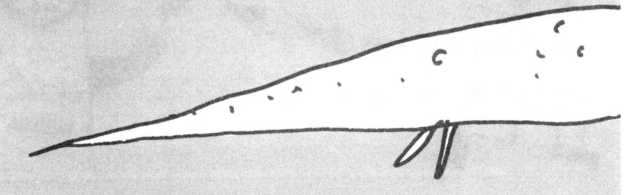

Everett (11)

The Ice Cream Shooting Machine

I dreamed that a big ice cream machine was mad at me. It bombarded me with ice cream cones. I was real scared, even though ice cream is soft. I had to run away or get hit.

EVERETT'S SOLUTION

I drew my dream, and to make myself safe enough to talk to the machine, I gave myself an invisible shield. I said, "What are you doing in my dream?" The machine said, "I spend my life making treats. I keep handing them out and you won't stick around when I need help." I said, " It's only ice cream but it hurts. You bombard me and I have to run away. " First I got the machine's point of view, then I gave him mine. Then we did some negotiating. . . . I agreed because it sounded like my mom. I said if she stopped bombarding me I'd stick around and help out one hour a day . . . and then I can go and play without feeling guilty. I don't really like this solution, but it was the only thing we could agree to or else I'd get bombarded all the time. Maybe an hour is too much . . . half an hour is better. I'm afraid if I agree to stick around, I'll never get to go and play.

COMMENTS

Everett drew the picture. From a position of safety behind the shield, he was able to talk to the Ice Cream Shooting Machine. When he heard what the machine had to say, he said he recognized the voice of his mother. Everett was able to hear both points of view, both complaints, and reach a settlement that was fair for both, even though he felt he couldn't trust the bargain.

DISCUSSION STARTERS

Why do you think he couldn't trust the bargain?

How does it feel to be bombarded?

How can children negotiate time for themselves to play when Mom never gets a rest?

How can parents negotiate help-time from kids without a hassle?

How do you get Mom to take a rest?

I didn't know what to do so I ran away I thought The Robot was going to capture me. He followed me until he caught up then I woke up.

COME BACK HERE!!!

Tim (11)

The Screaming Robot

I dreamed that a monster robot was chasing me all over the house with alarm signals screaming and lights flashing. I was so scared I started to scream. My own noise woke me up. I didn't dare go back to sleep.

TIM'S SOLUTION

I drew my dream and the way I made myself safe was to draw a turn-off switch on the robot so I could get it to stop flashing. Without juice it couldn't yell or flash its lights. Without juice, it couldn't even move. Then I closed my eyes to step back into the dream. Then I asked, "What are you doing in my dream?" And the robot said, "I just want you to play ball." I said, "If you want me to play ball, stop yelling and chasing me. You scare me when you chase me. I wish you were a little more human," and that gave me the idea to draw him a heart. Once I got it to stop yelling, we could talk. When it talked about being a robot and all the hard work it does, I felt sorry and offered to help out on condition that I could play without getting scolded. My dad's inside that robot I think. I gave him a new heart. I hope it works.

COMMENTS

Tim learned that if he could stand his ground he could negotiate a way for the robot and the chased boy to get some of what they both needed. He recognized the voice, and gave it a heart. When it sounded more reasonable, he agreed to "play ball" if the robot would agree to stop shouting and flashing.

DISCUSSION STARTERS

How is Dad like a robot?
What does it mean to be like a robot?
What does he mean "to play ball"?
If a robot gets a heart, is it still a robot?

39

THE RoboT cought UP TO mE AND TOLD ME THAT HE WANTED ME TO PLAY BALL

Joe (12)

The Green Dinosaur Monster

I dreamed this giant green dinosaur monster chased me all the way home. I ran and ran and just made it inside my house. I told my mother to look and see for herself. She said, "You're just imagining it." I looked out the window and it was gone. That made me feel like a liar. If my mother can't see something, she won't believe me.

JOE'S SOLUTION

I closed my eyes and let the picture speak to me. To make myself safe I spoke to the dinosaur through the keyhole. I told him I don't like being chased. I just made it into my house. I had to make the door extra strong. With my eyes closed, I could hear him better. I asked the dinosaur what he was doing in my dream. He said, "I'm scaring you." I told him my mom won't believe me. She says you're only in my imagination. I tell him no one can see him but me, and to me he is real. He says, "The things you imagine are the scariest things." Now that I found the courage to talk to him, he's not so scary. Now I

can see him, he is sort of real to me, like a
new friend.

COMMENTS

Joe faces three dilemmas in his dream—a
monster that's chasing him, a parent who
won't believe him, and a lively imagination
full of fears. In his solution, the monster
tells him the truth. Imaginary things are the
scariest ones and saying they are not real
doesn't help. When he and the monster
agree, they become friends and Joe's monster
becomes an ally.

DISCUSSION STARTERS

Do you have fears that adults pooh-pooh?
How does it feel when you can't explain why
   you're afraid?
What do you do when grown-ups don't believe you?
How do you deal with feelings that big and
   dangerous?

41

Ozzie (6)

Shouting In Space

I am a spaceman attached to a broken rocket. I'm out of communication with the transmitter. I will have to stay there until the spaceship blows up. I am shouting for help inside my mask. I can hardly hear inside my helmet, except a very faint voice says, "Come over here," but I can't, because I am attached. If I cut the cord I will die. If I take off my helmet to yell, I won't be able to breathe. I wake up thinking I am dead.

OZZIE'S SOLUTION

It was too scary to stay out in space waiting for the rocket to blow up. No one could hear or see me. I decided to pull myself back to the rocket to see if I could help the controller. I asked the rocket what to do. The rocket said, "My problem is too big for you to handle." The rocket said, "Get help." The guide said I should use my imagination to get help. So I invented a way . . . like SOS, I tapped dot-dot-dot/dash-dash-dash/dot-dot-dot (that means HELP in every language) to the faint voice, and he sent help. It was good that I came back to the rocket; it helped balance the ship so we could both think what to do. We got back to earth by using my imagination. We got help by signaling without words. I felt better. I wasn't dead. I wasn't as helpless as I thought. I'm glad I knew some Morse Code.

COMMENTS

Some nightmares are not about monsters, they are about feeling totally helpless. When dreams show you crying for HELP, it's a good idea to see how you can help yourself. It's good to know some other ways to communicate when you can't be seen or heard. Sometimes it helps to return to the problem, to see if you can help the broken part. And when a problem is too big to handle, try to find help from outside people.

43

DISCUSSION STARTERS

What does SOS mean? Can you tap it out?
If you were attached to something that's out of commission what could you do?
When problems in the home are bigger than you can handle, who can you turn to for help outside your family?
What helpers can a child get when parents are out of commission?

a prsan helpr me by saing com here
i sed i cant be casse
I'm attashed to tha
broken Rakit
I will haf to sta in
the spash ship blos up.

Shuting the Spas

Ron (11)

The Bike Race

44 I dream my best friend and I have a bike race. My friend is winning. His bike hits a stone. He falls off a cliff and dies. I win the race. I wake up glad to have won the race, but feel bad all day, especially when I see him at school. I'm afraid to tell him he died. I just can't stop thinking about it.

RON'S SOLUTION

I drew my dream. I don't want my friend to die, but I want to win the race. If he'd won, it wouldn't have been fair, because he had a new bike. His father wouldn't let him lend it. If it hadn't been for the accident, he would have beat me. I closed my eyes to ask the dream what it wants to tell me. It tells me I want to win, and I'm mad at the unfairness. To make a solution I had to use my imagination. I draw him back to life. I drew us back at the starting line. Then I drew in his father. We explained that to make the race fair we both had to ride the new bike. He said OK. He let me share the new bike because we are best friends. He timed the race. It was a tie.

COMMENTS

In a dream we can kill rivals and enemies without fear of reprisal. However, our waking conscience is often distressed by feelings of anxiety and guilt. The fear that we did such a thing in our dream worries us. We cannot face our friend. At a time like this, we welcome a more comfortable solution. The dream was also showing how unfair the race was, and how bad Ron felt that best friends couldn't share. Altering the circumstances of the dream issue is one way to change the situation. This dream may be showing Ron that it is easier to "bump off" your best friend than confront his father about sharing the bike. But with a little help from the guide, and a paper-stage rehearsal, it felt more comfortable to talk things over and get the father to help with the race than to have his friend fall over the cliff.

DISCUSSION STARTERS

Should best friends share everything?
When things aren't fair what can you do?
Have you wished someone dead and felt bad about it?
What do you do with guilty feelings?
Can you discuss problems with other people's parents?

Jan (13)

Hitler The Home Wrecker

46 ━━━━━━━━━━━━━━━━━━

I dreamed that Hitler is coming into my home, the way he wrecked my grandfather's home in Greece and then killed him. I am scared he will kill me. I want my mother to kill him so he will leave my mother and me alone.

JAN'S SOLUTION

[First Jan drew his mother killing Hitler, because he couldn't think of any other way to feel safe enough to ask what Hitler was doing in his dream.] Hitler said, "Killing won't stop me. I'm in charge of the world." My guide said try something else. Instead of killing Hitler, I tricked him: I locked Hitler in the cage. Then I closed my eyes so I could talk to him. "What's the big idea wrecking our home?" I said. He said, "Well I live here too, you know." Then he wasn't Hitler anymore, he was my stepfather. (Sometimes he acts just like Hitler: he wrecks our home, he takes my mom away, and I don't get things my way. . . It's always his way. I wish he'd get lost.) My solution was to get a psychiatrist to talk to him. . . . The psychiatrist told him I had some rights, too, because I knew my mom before he did. The psychiatrist helped, but I'm still mad because there is no psychiatrist, mom doesn't believe in it.

COMMENTS

Dreams about Hitler are very common. He has become a symbol of oppression, of destruction of human life and freedom, the ultimate and hateful controlling power. Nightmares about Hitler, or a similar inhuman being, often represent some controlling force in one's life that is beyond endurance. Killing seems to be the only solution and parents condone it in dreams, but note here, that Jan decides for himself that killing the enemy won't solve the problem. When children don't have any other ideas, I often suggest they call upon an expert or a specialist to help them find a more satisfactory or workable solution.

Jan finds help from a psychiatrist who defends his rights and agrees he should have preference over the invader of the family scene.

DISCUSSION STARTERS

Who would you talk to about feeling invaded?

What can kids do to protect their rights?

How does it feel to have a stepfather move in and take over?

How can you start to talk about this feeling with your mother or stepfather?

48

Joan (8)

Over My Head

I am with my daddy. He's divorced.
He takes me out in his boat. I fall overboard
and drown. He doesn't notice because he's
with his new girlfriend.

JOAN'S SOLUTION

I felt very angry at my dad for not even noticing me, not even when I was drowning. He's always talking to his girlfriend and forgetting about me. My solution to my picture was to swim over and get his attention. This time he heard me. (Next time he came to the house to take me for the weekend, I showed him this drawing. He laughed and said I had a pretty good sense of humor. That weekend he didn't ignore me so much. Everyone laughed at my picture, so I'm sorry I showed it.)

COMMENTS

Sometimes we don't even know how we feel until a dream gives us a picture that tells us. Sometimes dreams exaggerate the feeling just to wake us up and give us solutions to our real life problems. The wise part of Joan told the hurt part of Joan that if falling overboard didn't get Father's attention, she'd better try something else. She closed her eyes and asked her inner guide to help her find a better solution. She found the courage to talk it over with her father and showing him this picture helped, but she didn't think to tell him this was a private matter, so people wouldn't laugh at her drawing. To Joan it wasn't funny.

DISCUSSION STARTERS

How can you talk to your divorced fathers about jealousy?
How can you talk to your divorced mothers about your feelings?
How can you talk about feelings so people don't make them into a joke?

The Undelivered Birthday Cake

50

I had this dream since I was seven. I had it on and off for thirty-one years, especially after my dad died. It always makes me cry. It doesn't sound important, it's childish I know, but it keeps coming back. I'm as I was as a child, walking through the woods carrying a birthday cake. I made it myself for my father. I'm on my way to his castle to deliver it when some wild Indians jump out and scare me. . . . They destroy all my work, steal the cake. Every time I have this dream the Indians stop me. I'm so upset, I want so much to show my father this cake and tell him I love him. Now he is dead I'll never be able to do it. I always wake up crying. For years I thought this was a foolish dream.

MARJORY'S SOLUTION

I heard about this dream workshop. I was afraid to tell this silly dream out loud, but when we were asked if we had a recurring dream, I had to tell it. When I closed my eyes so I could imagine myself back in the woods, I became the little seven-year-old girl that used to be me. I held her hand. I gave her a stick to defend herself, I told her to shout at the Indians because TODAY, we were going to deliver the cake. Together we made those Indians stop dead in their tracks. "YOU LET US BY!" we said. "This cake is for the king and must be delivered whole." They shouted, "Only if you give us a piece of the cake." We agreed to save them a piece after we delivered it to Father. The minute they said OK, they turned into my younger brothers and sisters. I was the oldest of five, and the others always got to Dad first. Now it was my turn. We marched single file straight to my

father and gave him the beautiful cake. He was amazed that I made it myself and that I'd waited so long. I sat in his lap and never felt happier in all my life.

COMMENTS

Recurring dreams are like a messenger who keeps tapping on the door. When you dare to open the door and listen to the message, you may solve an old mystery and put the dream to rest. Marjory's embarrassment about a "foolish childish" dream bothered her until she took it seriously, until she worked out this solution. She wrote me several years later to tell me she had gotten married and how important this dream was to her. She felt that delivering the cake to her father, even though it was just a symbolic act, had a very lasting effect on her. She said it totally changed her feelings about her father. And talking to her father in this dream session had filled her with love and changed her life forever. She said, "I talk to him often when I feel left out or too embarrassed to express my feelings for fear of looking childish." Even when the people you love are gone, you can still visit them in your dreams and in your mind when you close your eyes.

DISCUSSION STARTERS

Have you had a recurring dream?
Have you been too shy to let someone know you love them?
Do you know how it feels to have to act grown up when you're the oldest and your feelings seem childish?

51

Sylvia (51)

The No Room

For years I've had this dream. I dream I hear the cry of a lost child somewhere inside my house. Each time I have this dream, I search the house for the crying child but never find it . . . until this workshop when I was asked to draw it and step back inside that scene and ask the lost child where I could find it. With my eyes closed I heard it say, "Look behind the mirror." In the mirror I recognized myself. It was me as a child, crying because I never took time to draw and paint, which I loved. I never had time for me.

SYLVIA'S SOLUTION

I closed my eyes and asked the little face in the mirror to forgive me. She said she'd been waiting for me to MAKE room for her to play for years. We both cried to think of how many years were lost. . . . "It's not too late. . . ,"she said, "let's begin today." On the way home from this workshop, I bought paints and brushes and promised we'd spend a part of every day from now on, playing with my new art materials. If I ever hear that crying child again I'll know to look in the mirror.

COMMENTS

Both Marjory and Sylvia had recurring dreams that lasted for years and years. The important lesson to learn from them is that it is never too late to make a change in your life. And childish things may be more important than you think.

53

DISCUSSION STARTERS

Have you a recurring dream you'd like to look at?
What "childish feelings" do you have sometimes?
Is there something you love to do that you don't make time for?

Kerry (10)

The Exploded Teacher

54

This guy was whipping me. He stole a car. The car hit a rock and exploded. He died. I was scared because this guy was really one of my teachers. He deserved something for whipping me and I was good and mad at him. In fact I hate his guts. But a dream like this really scares me because he was killed. I saw him explode. It was like it really happened, like I MADE IT HAPPEN.

HELP!

KERRY'S SOLUTION

After talking it over and getting the picture to speak, I realized the dream was saying I was mad enough to kill, and that is what the dream showed me, so I killed him with my imagination. But it felt so real it scared me. So if I was going to feel better and get this nightmare out of my head, I had to find a better solution. So instead of exploding him, I decided to send him to the army to be disciplined and punished for stealing a car. My second solution was to draw the principal into my picture and tell him that a mean bastard like this guy shouldn't be hired as a teacher. The principal I drew into my picture agreed with me, he said he just didn't know how bad he was. He didn't know that if the kids told on him he'd make them do push-ups like an army sergeant. Then I got a third solution. . . . I asked the guy why he was so mean, and he said because his parents beat him when he was a kid. . . . So then I drew in his parents and I told them it was against the law to beat kids. . . . Kids have rights, too. That made me understand his problem a little better. I still don't like him, but the bad dream is out of my head.

DIALOGUE

Kerry: Here's the picture. See this guy was whipping me. He stole a car—it hit a rock and exploded. He died. I was scared because it was really Rob, my gym teacher.
Guide: He was whipping you?
Kerry: Yeah, 'cause he likes to. . . . He's like a sergeant, I hate his guts, I'll grab his whip out of his hand and break it in half. [He draws the broken whip.]
Guide: What kind of help do you need? How will you make it less scary?
Kerry: I'm going to get the principal! He's big and he had a grudge on Rob anyway.
Guide: Good. Draw in the principal and ask what he thinks.
Kerry: [As the principal] "I want to talk to

Rob. Rob, you're FIRED." So he drives away in his car . . . and . . . explodes.

Guide: How does that make you feel?

Kerry: Well It got rid of him!!

Guide: Yes, but the way it happened in the dream scares you. Sounds like you don't want to wish death on anybody even if you are angry with them.

Kerry: That's right, but it's what happened in the dream.

Guide: The dream shows you how you feel—angry enough to kill or explode Rob. It's easy to kill in dreams, but if it bothers you afterwards, maybe you can try another way. It sounds like you know something about explosions.

Kerry: Yeah, I explode easily when I'm mad. And I'd explode him if I could.

Guide: That's what the dream is telling you?

Kerry: Yeah, the dream says I'm good and angry and ready to explode. He had this really fancy car that he stole. Then he crashed it. It's what happened, I didn't make it up! . . . or did I? It felt real in the dream. Did I make the dream?

Guide: How does this thought make you feel?

Kerry: So-so.

Guide: What would make you feel better?

Kerry: Well, let's see. We don't need to kill him, just whip him back. [Draws Rob being whipped.] That's Rob crying from the whipping. OK, that gets rid of him . . . but I can't handle it. . . . I can't get that explosion out of my head.

Guide: That gets rid of Rob, but not the problem of feeling whipped. What else could you do with your anger, so it won't hurt you nor kill him? Try another way to satisfy your feelings.

Kerry: Get whipped by the army.

Guide: You want the army to punish him?

Kerry: Yeah, send him to boot training. Let the sergeant whip him. [Closes his eyes and slams his arms around.]

Guide: What happened?

Kerry: Yes, the army whipped him good, wham, bam, slam!!!

Guide: How did that feel?

Kerry: Better. Maybe his parents used to whip him when he was a kid. Maybe I could go back and tell his parents that whipping made him mean and they shouldn't whip kids.

Guide: Try that.

Kerry: OK, I'm back a couple of years. OK. [Closes his eyes—allows the picture to materialize—opens his eyes.] Yes, they said they did whip him, now they say they're sorry, they won't do it again, so now he can stop whipping other kids.

Guide: So you don't need to destroy him? You need to understand him?

Kerry: I guess it will feel better in the end if I can understand him.

Guide: Does that help you get the bad picture out of your mind?

Kerry: Yeah, I guess it would feel better to understand him and to get the picture out of my mind.

COMMENTS

Haven't we all been shocked at the violence of our own rage in our dreams at some time or other? We scare ourselves sometimes, and the picture stays in our mind and bothers our conscience. Killing the enemy cuts off any chance of discovering the source or cure for our anger, and prevents resolution of the dream. I always suggest trying other ways to satisfy anger, but it's important to spend the anger first, in a safe way that does not hurt one's self nor violate another person. You can beat the devil out of a mattress with a stick, or chop wood, or close your eyes and take your tantrum out into space and let it explode where it will do no harm. When rage is spent, then look for alternative methods of satisfaction. It will feel better.

DISCUSSION STARTERS

Who can you speak to about feelings that scare you?

Name a safe way to let off steam when you're angry enough to kill.

If you hate someone, try to take time to understand why.

Albert (12)

The Sister-Napper

I heard footsteps and the rattling of chains, then this monster burst through the wall and grabbed my sister. I was so scared, I froze.

ALBERT'S SOLUTION

I feel like an ant and this guy is a giant. I couldn't think of anything to do at first. Then I grabbed the boat anchor and hooked it into his back. Then I asked him what he was doing, and he said he was scaring my sister. I agree she is a nuisance most of the time, but he didn't have to kill her. I like when she is a little scared; she needs me to defend her and that makes me feel grown up. He said he'd just scare her a little bit from now on. My solution to the picture was to make the giant smaller so I could handle the situation. I hate to feel like an ant. [Albert redrew the giant too small to frighten him, but still big enough to scare his sister a little.]

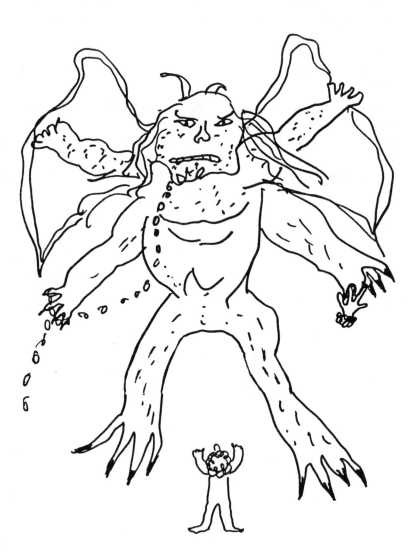

DIALOGUE

Guide: You were so frightened you couldn't move, but if you could have moved what would you have done?

Albert: I'd have taken the boat anchor and hooked it into his back. [Albert draws an anchor in the giant's back.]

Guide: What is your sister saying?

Albert: "Help, I feel helpless, the man is a giant."

Guide: If you could get help, what would you do?

Albert: She thinks I can save her, but there is nothing I can do. Look I'm an ant, and he's got her. Even though my sister is a nuisance most of the time, I don't want to see her killed.

Guide: If you could talk to him what would you say?

Albert: I'd advise him to scare her a little, but not to scare me.

Guide: What happens when your sister is a little scared?

Albert: She makes me defend her. I kind of like that, but not when big monsters are around. Then I can't handle it.

Guide: How does it feel when you can't handle it?

Albert: It makes me feel very small.

COMMENTS

When the dreamer is unable to move, it helps to ask what they would do if they could move. This as-if question sort of tricks a person into action despite the paralysis. Children are often frightened by their own feelings of fear, as well as the feeling of being paralyzed and powerless, especially when they think someone is depending on them to defend or save them. If we know it's not real, we can all enjoy playing the hero, but if a real big man kidnapped our sister we'd be too scared to move. The dream tells the truth.

DISCUSSION STARTERS

Is there someone you might have to save and fear you couldn't?

If someone is in danger and the job is too big for you, do you know how to get help?

Has your teasing ever gone so far you scare yourself?

HELP I'M TRAPPED IN THE WORLD

Thad (11)

Trapped in the World

There is a lot of confusion everywhere. Everything is trying to get all the people killed. I am always running away from it. I have to go down out of the way and keep saying to myself how impossible it is for all this confusion . . . all the other people are all dead . . . it would be impossible for you to find a way out . . . so that's the problem. I'm trapped in there . . . trapped in the world.

THAD'S SOLUTION

I felt so trapped at first, I had to hide in a box so I could think what to do. Then my imagination started working and I imagined being in Arizona where it's peaceful, where my mind could rest from all this confusion. Then I didn't feel so scared. I drew this picture of the mesas and the mountains to put on my wall so when things get too confusing I can go there in my mind. I could talk to the monster by telephone. I asked him why he came into my dream. He said he gets angry when he wants to be left alone. He said he is greedy because he is really lonely and doesn't know how to make friends. He said it wouldn't kill me to talk to him instead of running away scared . . . so we talked and he got less scary. He said he had to mess up . . . that's the only way he knew how to get some attention. My solution was to teach him how to make friends, step-by-step. I also had to show him some of the good things he's got to be thankful for, like the beautiful ocean, the Sierras, the green grass. It will help him when he feels confused, and I have a picture to put on my wall to remind him.

DIALOGUE

Guide: I see you certainly do look like you feel trapped in confusion. Is it everywhere?

Thad: No, it's just in that part, but I can't get out . . . I can't just hop on a plane to somewhere else.

Guide: Let's see what might help you. How can you make yourself safe enough to go into this picture and help the trapped self?

Thad: I could find a box [draws a box] and hide inside it so I can think. But not for long or I can't breathe.

Guide: You're in charge of the time . . . So whatever feels safe . . . be very kind to that trapped boy. How will you begin to help him find a safe place?

Thad: I'll have to go inside my head . . . I can think of a place I really like in Arizona.

Guide: Close your eyes and go there. . . . Give your trapped boy a little rest from the confusion.

Thad: OK, I'm there. . . . It's very flat all around and all of a sudden there is a very thin mesa that seems to be balanced very lightly, and everything is very flat for miles around and then there's another mesa, and another, and a soft wind is really nice.

Guide: Get a good deep breath of all that peacefulness and balance. Really take it into your lungs and heart, into all the

61

troubled places, so it feels like you're there in the soft wind and sun, so you can feel it.

Thad: Right . . . because it's getting hot. It is hot, that's real. I can feel it on my skin.

Guide: That's something you can do for yourself whenever confusion gets to be too much for you.

Thad: I also like the idea of leaves all over a big green lawn. That helps me too.

Guide: How about drawing these safe places and hanging them up in your room so you can remember this when you feel trapped in the world? [Thad draws the mesas.]

Guide: While you're in this safe place, is there anything you'd like to say to the monster or the confusion?

Thad: I can talk to him long distance. He is saying "Nothing can stop me."

Guide: Ask what he wants.

Thad: He wants death.

Guide: Ask what else he would settle for. Violence is a waste of people and the good earth.

Thad: He wants the world and all the buildings.

Guide: What do you think is wrong with him that makes him so destructive and greedy?

Thad: [Closes his eyes . . . long silence.] Might be lonely.

Guide: See if that's it. . . . Listen some more.

Thad: That's it . . . he's lonely.

Guide: How can you help the lonely part of him?

Thad: Make some friends.

Guide: Can you show him? . . . Close your eyes and see what making friends looks like.

Thad: Well, I see I'd start by first not just running away because you're scared of him, because you're assuming that he's going to kill you.

Guide: He wants you to dare to stay a minute, listen, and not assume he's going to kill you?

Thad: That's what he wants.

Guide: Would you be able to try that?

Thad: Yes, well, I could, but it doesn't really want to be friends. It wants to be left alone . . . it likes to be free.

Guide: I see. It's important to understand exactly what someone wants and not assume you know?

Thad: I could try to leave it alone. After it messes up, it will go away.

Guide: First it has to mess up?

Thad: Yeah . . . Those mess-ups are a pain.

Guide: Do you think there is a way for it to get freedom and attention without messing up? Bring your best wisdom in to help you give him some advice.

Thad: Show 'em how to make friends?

Guide: Can you show him how?

Thad: I'm not very good at that. . . . I'd tell him my name.

Guide: You'd find the courage to tell him your name. That's a good start. Do you want to tell him how he scares you?

Thad: No, he couldn't take that from me . . . others can tell him . . . you couldn't get to him . . . if you got that close he'd get you.

Guide: Does he know Arizona?

Thad: No, but I can show him what he has got here.

Guide: What has he got?

Thad: He's got the ocean . . . he disappeared the minute I said that. . . . I don't think I have a solution . . . just a more cheerful picture. That helps though.

Guide: Are you still in the box?

Thad: No, I got out of it when I went to Arizona.

62

COMMENTS

Thad's dream depicts a world of total destruction, helplessness, and confusion. It is also a world where adults are no help. To help him gain power over the dream, I suggested he find a safe place, somewhere he could get away from all the war planes and fire-breathing confusion. From a position of safety, he could begin to sort out the problem and deal with the dream. Sometimes there are no real solutions, but at least Thad was able to look at his fear, change his position. He saw, too, that when a creature feels lonely and isn't very good at making friends, the world can be a disastrous place. As guide, one needs to be sensitive to the dreamer's readiness to approach danger and consider change. Do not take the dreamer any further than feels safe to them. Thad needed lots of time before he could speak to his monster, and even then, the contact was tentative, and in the end, he withdrew. Evidently, that was all he could handle for the moment. The guide must be satisfied that even changing one small aspect of the nightmare defuses the total impact of the fear. As it was, Thad was able to talk a little bit about loneliness, making friends, and "messing up" as an ineffective way of getting attention.

DISCUSSION STARTERS

Can you find a safe place inside?
When you are lonely, how can you begin to make friends?
Close your eyes and create a safe place inside your mind, or a think-shelter to rest in.
Do you ever "mess up" in order to get attention?

63

Joanna (11)

The Unacceptable Divorce

This dream started at the beach. My mom and dad began arguing, just a little bit. When we came home they were really arguing, getting really mad at each other. . . . Then they got divorced. I was crying and crying. I couldn't handle it. Then Mom came and gave me a hug, and my dog got killed and that was too awful to bear. I couldn't handle that either. Then we went back to the beach and that was hysterical. All the leaves on all the trees turned black everywhere. . . . Nothing was right when Mom left. . . . Then when Mom came back, everything turned green again. Then they're on this hill and I'm here with these people from school and with my old friends, and the earth cracked open and started eating everybody. I was on the other side and couldn't help them. I couldn't do anything about them. I just couldn't handle it most of the time.

JOANNA'S SOLUTION

It makes me cry to have to think about this dream. I had to put all the tears in my picture. I needed help. It was all too much to cope with. To find some comfort, I decided to draw my grandmother. I closed my eyes and listened to see what she'd say and she said, "Well, it's not the end of the world." To help my friends, I drew in a trampoline so they could bounce back up. Then I asked my crying self, "What would help you?" She said, "If my parents can't get along they can still be friends." So I had my father say, "I still love you but I can't live with you," and my mother say, "OK, now we can respect one another and stop fighting." Then I drew in my father saying, "I'm sorry, I didn't mean to hurt you." Then the crying me says, "I am very, very sad, but it's not the end of the world. Maybe I can begin to accept the idea. At least I can talk with my grandmother. I can live with her maybe." My dog says, "I am hurt but not dead." I don't like this dream, but I can handle it better.

DIALOGUE

Joanna: [Begins to cry; points to the tears in her picture.] They're getting divorced.

Guide: I see lots and lots of tears. This dream certainly is showing you how sad you feel.

Joanna: Yes. . . . It's totally unacceptable. It makes me remember that I just couldn't do anything to stop it.

Guide: If you could now, what would you do to help your crying self in your picture?

Joanna: If somehow I could make my friends land softly so they don't get eaten.

Guide: Can you think of a way? Use your imagination.

Joanna: Well . . . I could put a trampoline down in the crack so they'd bounce.

Guide: Try that.

Joanna: [Draws in a trampoline.] Now they can bounce back.

Guide: You have found a way to help them bounce back! How does that feel?

Joanna: That's better.

Guide: A lot like life, full of things that look totally unacceptable that we can't change, then you find a way to bounce back. What else would help?

Joanna: For divorce not to happen.

Guide: Of course, but let's work with the dream situation as you dreamed it. What would have to happen for you to bounce back?

Joanna: It would help if they could still be friends, if parents can't live together but are still friends. . .

Guide: How will you say that here on your drawing?

Joanna: Um . . . they're fighting together all the time.

Guide: Give them some words.

Joanna: [Writes in father's balloon.] "I love you but I can't live with you."

Guide: What's mother say?

Joanna: "All right. We won't live together but we will respect one another; we won't fight."

Guide: Close your eyes again and see what else you'd like to hear that would help you.

Joanna: He needs to say, "I'm sorry, I didn't mean to hurt you."

Guide: Close your eyes and see what Joanna says.

Joanna: [Long silence.] She says, "I'm very, very sad, but I could begin to accept the idea."

Guide: It's hard to consider your world breaking up when that's all you've ever known. How could you help this crying part of yourself, what would comfort her? [Joanna is trying not to cry, wiping tears away.] First she needs to cry. I see lots and lots of tears and that helps. Can you comfort her in this drawing? After she stops crying she might think of something or someone who could comfort her.

Joanna: She could go off to college.

Guide: How many years before you go to college?

Joanna: Six years.

Guide: What are you going to do while you're waiting?

Joanna: I could live with my grandmother.

Guide: Put your grandmother into your picture. See what she says.

Joanna: [Draws in a lively colorful young grandmother with red shirt and green slacks.]

Guide: What's she saying?

Joanna: "It's not the end of the world."

Guide: Say it again so everyone hears it.

Joanna: "IT'S NOT THE END OF THE WORLD."

66

Guide: Now what about the dog?

Joanna: I don't have the slightest idea who did that. My mom maybe, but she loves the dog.

Guide: Close your eyes and ask the dog what's going on.

Joanna: The dog says she doesn't feel dead but she's very hurt. She says she's innocent. She says I could take away the axe and burn it.

Guide: Who else is feeling innocent like the dog?

Joanna: My mom I guess. I don't know.

Guide: Who feels axed?

Joanna: I guess I do, but it's probably my fault.

Guide: So if it's your fault and you also feel innocent, that could feel confusing.

Joanna: That's it: I'm really confused.

Guide: How will you help the dog in the picture?

Joanna: [Writes in the dog's bubble, "I'm hurt but not axed."]

Guide: You've really done some hard work. How does this feel?

Joanna: I'm relieved, but I still can't accept that my parents are divorced in my dream, I'm afraid they really will. That's the problem. It just couldn't happen and it did happen in my dream and I feel to blame.

Guide: Dreams have a way of rehearsing some of the things we fear. Perhaps it's a way of experiencing things that could possibly happen. Dreams introduce us to change sometimes before it happens. If it should happen, you'd feel better knowing that you were not to blame, that it's not the end of the world, and that your grandmother could comfort you and be of help.

Joanna: Yes. I'd like my dad to say that it's not my fault. [Writes it in his balloon.]

Guide: Remember, dreaming something doesn't make it happen. Dreaming just brings up a worry so your conscious mind can get acquainted with it. Sometimes dreams do foretell the future, but whatever happens, you are not to blame and you do have some options to draw strength from. It's not the end of the world.

COMMENTS

67

There were many elements to consider about this one dream, but I tried to stick to the techniques, acknowledging the strong feelings of the girl, who was obviously very upset. I offered reassurance; we stayed with the dream situation and worked with the various parts of it. She used the closing of the eyes to hear the wisdom from within, and I encouraged her to dialogue with the different characters, including the dog. (Animals often reflect some aspect of ourselves.) For most children, even the idea of divorce is unacceptable. But in these times, divorce is all around us, and children are rarely consulted until it's upon them. It helps if they have some neutral party to go to for support during the period of upset and transition, especially when the divorce is not an amicable one. In Joanna's school there was such a high percentage of divorced parents that the children put together a book to express their feelings and their roles in divorce.

DISCUSSION STARTERS

Do you have someone to talk to outside your family?

No child is fully to blame for the adults' relationship, but kids are apt to get squeezed in the middle. If you feel you are to blame, can you talk about it?

Is divorce a reality in your family, or is it something you are worried about?

Can you express feelings instead of worrying in silence?

Can you get parents to listen when you need to tell them how you feel?

What are some things you can do to make yourself more independent?

Martha (8)

Hiding from Hitler

We have all been studying about Hitler and the Jews at school. One night I dreamed I was Jewish. All our neighborhood (which is Jewish except for us) took turns watching for Hitler. One day, Hitler was coming. Like everybody else, I ran to the pond to hold my breath under water. All of a sudden, I noticed my cat following me. I couldn't leave her behind for Hitler to kill. If she follows me, she'd give me away and we'd both be killed. Fortunately it was a false alarm. So the next day, my cat was put to sleep. Then Hitler came again and we all ran. We heard the marching boots, then my mother called my name and I woke up. I heard banging and ran downstairs. My father was still up. He said the noise was my heart beating. My cat came and rubbed my leg; everything was OK. But I felt bad. In Germany it was NO DREAM.

MARTHA'S SOLUTION

I closed my eyes and let the picture speak. The cat said, "Save me. Don't put me to sleep, I'm innocent." So I drew her a safe place so she didn't have to be put away. Then Hitler said he ruled the world, and I said, "No, you don't—not if no one follows your orders." I think we have to teach people to think for themselves so people like Hitler never get into power again. I decided to draw myself as a teacher and I would teach kids. We have to start here in school and at home and stop persecution when it's little so it never gets big enough to rule the world. I'll probably be a teacher when I grow up.

COMMENTS

We discussed this in class. If one race or even one person in the school is being persecuted, what can we do? Hide? Breathe under water? Ask to be saved, because "I'm not one of them . . . it's not my worry?". . . Kill an innocent cat that might betray your hiding place? . . . NO we agreed. It has to be everybody's worry.

Martha's dream contains so many complex emotions one must marvel at a dream that can bring them all together in one small paragraph. She must face misidentification, persecution, the death of innocence. She also faces the moral dilemma of saving herself at the expense of others who are innocent. I am constantly stunned at the sophistication of children's dreams. In their dreams they experience all the complex emotions that adults experience, though they may lack the vocabulary to articulate their feelings. I was hard-pressed to help Martha, but she seems to have found her own way.

DISCUSSION STARTERS

What is persecution?
Have you ever been persecuted? How did it feel?
When we see unfair treatment going on in school or at home, what can we do about it?

Todd (12)

Death Comes in My Room

This is a story of death. He comes to my room with red eyes. It started when I was six years old. He's scary and black and comes often. At night he's much scarier than this drawing. He bothers me almost every night.

TODD'S SOLUTION

At first I felt scared to draw death, but I found I was able to talk to him. I wouldn't want to do it alone but it was daylight and we did it in class. I told him I respect him now and I'm glad he didn't get my little brother. I told him he doesn't need to come every night so I can't sleep. I didn't realize that my six-year-old self in the picture needed some attention, I found that out when I closed my eyes. Because even though he didn't get headlines in the paper like my big brother, he (I) did help save my little brother by running to get Mom. I guess I felt unnoticed.

DIALOGUE

Todd: It's hard to draw death as scary as he really is in my dream.

Guide: What do you know about death?

Todd: Lots of things died in my room: guinea pigs and gerbils, and my little brother almost died when he choked on a carrot.

Guide: Would you draw that story so we can see it. Would you like to talk to the people in it?

Todd: [Draws his fourteen-year-old brother reading to him and his four-year-old brother in bed. His little brother's face is blue.] We noticed he wasn't talking, he looked funny. I ran for help.

Guide: Would you draw what happened next.

Todd: [Draws this scene.] While I was gone to get Mom, my big brother did the Heimlich maneuver on him and he began to breathe. [Draws the Heimlich maneuver.]

Guide: Draw what happened next.

Todd: My brother got headlines in the newspaper. [Todd draws the headlines.]

Guide: How did it feel to have your brother get all the attention?

Todd: Well he saved his life.

Guide: What do you think that six-year-old boy in your dream deserves? Close your eyes and ask him what he wants.

Todd: He says he wants some attention.

Guide: You mean he deserves some credit for helping to save his brother's life?

Todd: A little. He ran to get Mom.

Guide: Draw the little six-year-old you getting what he deserves. Can you close your eyes and see that scene?

Todd: Uh huh. He's getting hugged.

Guide: Good. Close your eyes and ask him if that's enough to get death to stop visiting you at night.

Todd: Not really.

Guide: Close your eyes and see what else he needs.

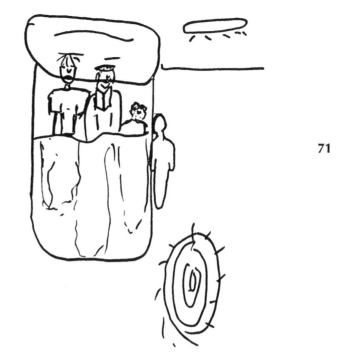

Heimlich maneuver

72

Todd: He needs a little more attention.

Guide: Could you give that six-year-old part of yourself some more attention. Doesn't he deserve your hug, too?

Todd: That's hard.

Guide: Why?

Todd: Just hard to draw.

Guide: Give it a try. Remember, he's only six and you are now twelve. He was left out of the drama and deserved a place in it. He was the first to run for help. Six is very young to have such a close visit from death. Many people don't experience that until much later in life. See if you can tell death that you have learned to respect him, but you don't need him to visit you every night. See if you can draw yourself comforting that scared six-year-old and give him the attention he deserves so he can grow up too. [When I came back to see Todd, he had several discarded drawings of a stiff embrace. The drawing he kept was one of heads together—he was too embarrassed to hug himself, but he did tell himself he'd done a good job for a six-year-old.]

COMMENTS

Death encounters in childhood are very so-
bering. Few of us prepare our children at all.
We think by protecting them from it they are
spared. In Italy, my son's first-grade reader
had many stories about the death of grandparents, babies, other relatives, and animals.
I was shocked at first, but now I think it
wiser than our avoidance of the subject. It
helps to talk about death before it confronts
us, especially when it comes close to home.

  I use guided imagery, especially when we
need wisdom from a higher source. Wisdom
and good counsel often come to us in the
form of an animal. The summer that Todd
was with me, we'd end the class with a
thought to grow on. I would ask the group to
allow wisdom to take any form it wished and
give them a message for the day. The group
had been talking about death dreams. Todd's
wisdom came in the form of a big Clydesdale
horse who showed him how to stand and
dare to be bold and strong. On another day,
his wisdom came to him in the form of a red
fox who said not to be so fearful and serious—to run, to play, to dare to love life. Are
we not our own best guides!

DISCUSSION STARTERS

Did you ever have a pet that died?
Who can you talk to about death?
What does death mean in your family?
Would we have life if we didn't have death?
What did the red fox mean?
When is death a blessing?

73

DEATH

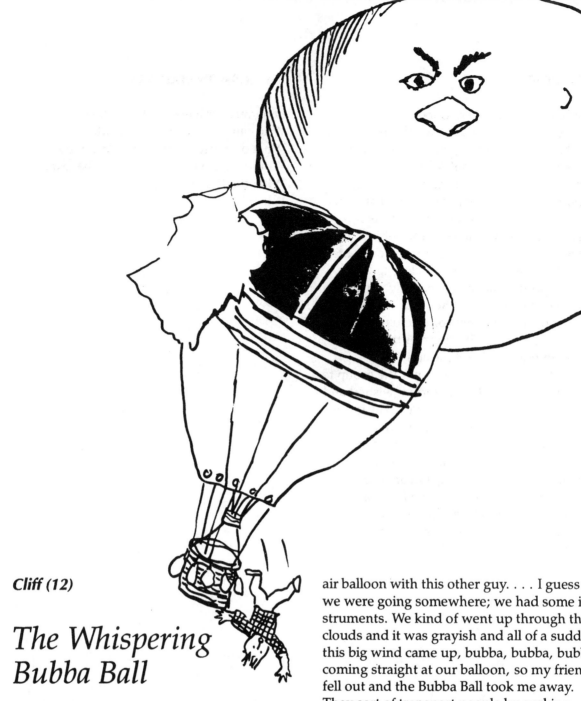

Cliff (12)

The Whispering Bubba Ball

These dreams are like the Hardy Boy books or Nancy Drew stories. They come in a series of adventures. I used to have them often, but this one I remember best, I had it when I was about seven. This giant thing that looks like a sort of ball with no arms or legs, just eyes and mouth, comes up to you and clings to your neck when you sleep, and says, "Bubba, bubba, bubba." It tickled, but it was scary for some reason. Here I am in this hot air balloon with this other guy. . . . I guess we were going somewhere; we had some instruments. We kind of went up through the clouds and it was grayish and all of a sudden this big wind came up, bubba, bubba, bubba, coming straight at our balloon, so my friend fell out and the Bubba Ball took me away. They sort of transport people by sucking them up inside themselves, and carrying them off. It was flesh-colored, kind of transparent like a human, and it took me to this place called Bad Dream Land, where all bad dreams come from. There were a lot of big tents and Bubba Balls were sitting around lifting weights and doing punching bags. Kids get changed before they come out of the training camp. That's why I was up there—to get changed. If I didn't do it, something would happen to me. It was scary.

CLIFF'S SOLUTION

It took me a lot of thinking to find a good solution. I tried a lot of things. First I had to draw in a parachute for my friend to land without killing himself. I couldn't control the Bubba Ball, so I went and found the director of Bubba Balls who had some authority. He gave me a job and agreed to make the Bubba Ball lay off for a year on a trial basis while I grew my own independent wings. That made me feel real good. The controller respects me now, so I don't need to escape the job he gave me. See in the picture I'm growing wings so I can fly on my own.

DIALOGUE

Guide: Can you give the Bubba Ball a voice?
Cliff: It doesn't speak. It just says, "Bubba, bubba."
Guide: Why do you think it came?
Cliff: It wanted me to go off to this place. It wanted to see if I was going to get changed and take this job. I didn't really want to, but it had some big plan for me. I was going to say OK, but then when it wasn't looking, I was going to escape somehow. . . . Then I woke up. It was very scary . . . like all the Bubbas were being very nice to me . . . smiling and all. . . . You can't really do anything against them. Speaking about them makes them get bigger. If you let them inflate, you have some extra time to

get away. That keeps them busy so they don't come back for a little while at least.
Guide: That gave you a little time?
Cliff: Yeah, I'm not very stable in this balloon; they are hard to maneuver. . . . I mean we can't just float around. I'll draw some sandbags, that will stabilize us. . . . A plane would be a better vehicle. I could draw that on a separate sheet. [He draws a plane on a new sheet.] But that's the false dream when you change it. I don't know much about dreams—nothing scientific— but there are false dreams and real ones. This was a real one because it woke me up.
Guide: So what are you doing to empower yourself in the "real" dream?
Cliff: I'm getting a plane so I can zero out of the picture. Bubbas are not particularly fast. I tried once in one of my dreams to reason with it . . . hum.
Guide: Close your eyes and look inside the Bubba Ball and give it a voice. See what the story is, why it comes into your dream.
Cliff: Well, it usually comes and does what others want it to do: sometimes it has a mind of its own. It came this time because it had to transport me to this other place. It sort of had orders from somewhere.
Guide: Could you find out where the orders are coming from?
Cliff: From the manager, the guy who runs the training camp. . . . It's also kind of like a club . . . it's kind of a messenger.
Guide: The Bubba Ball is a messenger?
Cliff: Not all the time.

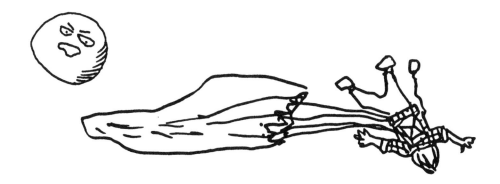

Guide: Is there anything you'd like to say to the messenger?

Cliff: Whatever . . . he . . . she . . . whatever it is, it took me to a place and we were talking about hours and stuff. . . . I was going to join up, then escape when I saw the chance.

Guide: What's it feel like when this Bubba Ball comes?

Cliff: Sometimes it's awful. It feels like it's going to create a pressure in my head, in my body, and whenever that happens, I know that the Bubba Ball or something else bad is going to happen.

Guide: It has a strong effect on you? What can you do?

Cliff: In some dreams I've tried doctors, holding my breath. Sometimes it works.

Guide: Bring your best wisdom in now to guide you. Close your eyes and listen. What would that advice be?

Cliff: "Give him more authority," it says . . . but I'm somehow brainwashed by the Bubba Ball, 'cause they're very smart.

Guide: Who should get more authority?

Cliff: This messenger would have to give me more authority over the Bubba Ball and then that's all I need.

Guide: How are you going to begin? Can you handle it?

Cliff: I don't know. If I was not exactly hired, but given some branch of management, like a test period.

Guide: What seems reasonable?

Cliff: I don't know . . . a year?

Guide: You could have control for a year on trial?

Cliff: Yes, some freedom from the Bubba Ball.

Guide: How does that feel?

Cliff: Isn't that like brainwashing? My father told me that people can work on your mind and brainwash you.

Guide: It sounds here more like empowering yourself. You dared to ask for more authority.

Cliff: Well, Bubba Balls don't really communicate very easily, but if I got this power, this authority, then I would be able to get free.

Guide: Can you close your eyes and see yourself trying this.

Cliff: [Closes his eyes. . . . Silence.] I ran out in the airplane. I go off to the back and I say I need some authority because these Bubba Balls are coming into my dreams too often.

Guide: What did the messenger say?

Cliff: He said, "Alright. You can have it free for a limited time." He'll tell the Bubba

Balls to take a year off. . . . They can be around, but not to blow up my balloon. . . I guess I got that authority. Right now I can give some orders.

Guide: How does that feel?

Cliff: It feels better.

Guide: Can you draw a symbol of authority into your picture?

Cliff: Yeah . . . like wings . . . with wings I don't need a balloon to hold me up. [He drew a parachute on his friend so his friend could land safely, and he drew wings for himself.]

COMMENTS

In puberty, we feel lots of strange things and can't quite figure them out or know just when we will have to face the truth called sex. Seduction, independence, fear, inadequacy, urges, curiosity, and adventure are all mixed up, and the confusion over sexuality frequently manifests itself in dreams. Although the sexual overtones of Cliff's dream seemed obvious to me, I knew it would probably not be necessary to dwell there. If we are to respect a dream, we must leave it as it comes and work with the disguises it has chosen. I feel, especially when working with children, that the dreamer should decide what to look at and what to do. As the guide, I simply try to help the child empower themselves at whatever level they choose to handle. Cliff chose to negotiate a deal around the issue of responsibility and authority, gave himself a trial period to see if he was ready for it, and started to grow wings of independence.

DISCUSSION STARTERS

Authority has its price. What is the price Cliff is ready to pay?

Is the price of independence taking more responsibility?

What do you think the Bubba Ball is whispering?

We fight feeling controlled by authority, yet we feel like we're floating and unstable without it. How would you balance this?

77

Jack (12)

The Christmas Tree Ornament

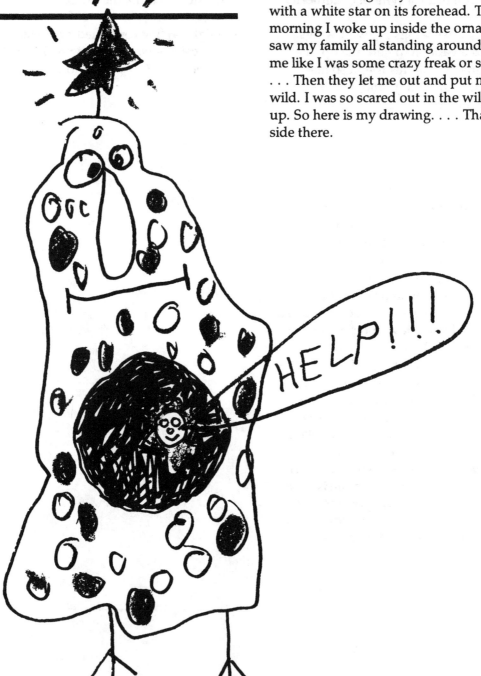

I had this dream when I was two and a half. I remembered it for ten years, and it still scares me. I was knocking the ground by this big rock and something started to grow like a Christmas tree. Then it came to life and walked upstairs. Then it grew a big giant ornament like a big belly button. It was blue with a white star on its forehead. The next morning I woke up inside the ornament and saw my family all standing around staring at me like I was some crazy freak or something. . . . Then they let me out and put me in the wild. I was so scared out in the wild I woke up. So here is my drawing. . . . That's me inside there.

JACK'S SOLUTION

I closed my eyes and talked to the little me inside the ornament. Little me said he was scared to get out, so he grew inside the ornament. He grew too big to get out. But now with the help of the time machine, I helped him burst out. I helped him by drawing him some feet so that he could stand on his own legs; then he wasn't so scared to get out. Then I got my mother and we got him a baby tree to keep him company and special juices to make him grow feet. Now that I've made up a solution, I feel much better.

DIALOGUE

Guide: Close your eyes and go back into the dream picture and ask this little person what he wants.

Jack: I'm inside here; I'm two and a half. I want to get out, but I'm too big and I'm scared. . . . See. . . . I became a monster.

Guide: Ask the monster to guide you so you can help him get out.

Jack: He says get a time machine. It's the only way.

Guide: Try that.

Jack: [Draws in the time machine.] OK, I've

got a time machine. I go back a couple of years. OK, now I'll have to smash open the ornament.

Guide: Go easy . . . so he won't get hurt.

Jack: Yeah, I have to crack it first so he won't get hurt. He's getting out, going downstairs to get his mother. Now I'll talk to the Christmas tree . . . find out what it wants. It wants a baby Christmas tree . . . wants to possess him into a baby . . . but he doesn't want that . . . so maybe I should sacrifice myself. . . .

Guide: You said you were the star. What else could you do besides sacrifice yourself?

Jack: I'll go outside and chop down a baby tree and decorate it and put it inside the big ball. I'll put it in special Christmas tree juices so it can grow feet . . . then everybody's happy . . . The End.

Guide: Are you showing the little baby star how to grow up outside the ornament before he gets too big?

Jack: Yeah, I guess I could show him since I'm the star and I got out without getting broken. Then I don't need to sacrifice. [Draws baby getting out of ornament.] You know what happened after that? My grandmother came and destroyed our real Christmas tree because she thinks if you have a bad dream you should destroy the thing you dream about. But I think this is a better way.

COMMENT

What on earth is this about? A pregnant Christmas tree, birth, getting too big to get out, the birth of a sibling, wanting to remain the baby, finding one's own feet to stand on, being treated like an ornament. We did not have time to find out, and this was not a therapy session—but I did know that early traumas, losing one's star place in the family, childhood misunderstandings of birth and cesarean sections, adult talk we don't understand can leave us with strange images. Part of us may be stuck back in those scrambled impressions and feelings that are not yet updated. It helps to go back in time and unstick the stuck part. Dreams often show them to us in strange ways. [I consider recurring dreams an invitation to deal with a stuck mind-set or to unscramble an old childhood myth that may not be true but is nevertheless firmly stuck.] It appears that two-year-old Jack had some confusion over the birth process and "special juices that make things grow" perhaps like sperm. He felt he had turned into a monster, and he also learned something about sacrifice, as many first children do when there's a new baby in a family.

In one session with a child, understanding is not always the best goal. I prefer that the child satisfy their own needs rather than my curiosity. There are always many possible directions to take, but it is safest to ask the child what direction interests them. And follow patiently.

Jack's solution allowed him to grow legs, get out of the ornament without getting hurt, and teach the baby tree how to do it rather than sacrificing himself or remaining a monster. If you will keep abreast of the child's feelings at every move, that is your best guide . . . to satisfy feelings is to feel better.

DISCUSSION STARTERS

What is it like to feel like an ornament?
What does a Christmas tree symbolize?
If you can't find your own feet what happens to you?
Do your grandparents have any superstitions?

What about "special juices that make things grow." [Only if you're ready to discuss the facts of life.]

Mindy (5)

The Tractor and the Baby Tree

I dreamed that a big tractor with heavy tires came right by, very close, and ran right over a baby tree. It wasn't very nice.

MINDY'S SOLUTION

Seeing my picture of the baby tree all smashed made me feel very sad. I asked the picture to talk and the baby tree said to the tractor, "Why did you do that? I don't like you for smashing me down. After all, I am planted here and can't move out of your way." Then the tractor said, "I'm more important than a baby tree. I have to do my work and you are in my way." The only solution I could think of was to draw a little house to protect the tree until it gets big enough to offer the tractor shade; then they could be friends. I put a skylight in the roof so that the tree gets sunlight.

DIALOGUE

Guide: Now that you've drawn it, let's find out what is going on. Close your eyes and let the tree and the tractor speak, what do they say?

Mindy: The tree says, "I was planted here and can't move. You should look out where you go." The tractor says, "What do I care! I didn't ask you to be planted there. What do I care about little trees?" The tree says, "I am not very big or strong yet. You might mow right over me with your big tire." The tractor says, "What do I care? You're in my way. I've got work to do."

Guide: How does that make you feel? [Mindy cries.] What kind of solution are you going to try to help the little tree? Close your eyes and see the tree getting protection.

Mindy: Well . . . [long pause with eyes closed] . . . I see the tree inside walls. I could draw a little house around the baby tree until it gets a stronger trunk. If I make a glass roof it can get light. The tractor respects houses. [She draws a house around the tree.]

Guide: Close your eyes and see how that is working out.

Mindy: [Closes eyes, long silence.] He doesn't run into the house. The tree says, "Humm. Maybe when I get bigger I can give the tractor some shade to rest under, and he'll make friends." I'm not so scared of him anymore. But sometimes I feel just like that little tree.

Guide: It sounds like you know how it feels to be nearly mowed down.

Mindy: Yes . . . that's it, it doesn't feel very nice.

Guide: Can you tell that to the tractor or to someone else, the next time you feel mowed down? Maybe in your waking life you could use the tree's message as a signal to speak up and remind people that you have feelings, too. What is the message from this dream?

Mindy: I have feelings, too?

COMMENTS

We know that many babies come into the world unplanned, even unwanted, cursed, and blamed: welcome is often withheld throughout pregnancy and even long into childhood. Don't for a minute think children are ignorant of these feelings. Even if they are unexpressed reservations, or if they change to positive feelings after birth, I am convinced we carry some knowledge of this in our body memory from the reaction of the muscles in the womb and the blood system that joins us to our maternal hostess. Words may be unavailable to prove this, but images such as Mindy found in her dream are common in therapeutic work. If you feel it, it is real! Wherever they come from, symbolic feelings are important to listen to. The helplessness of a rooted tree versus the brutish

recklessness of a man-powered tractor describes something not all five-year-olds understand instinctively. Only those who share the feelings will recognize it. The emergency and style of urgency is important to note. Unable to escape attack, this tree seems to be rooted in the tractor's path. We can't change the circumstances of our position at birth or in childhood, but we can learn to strengthen and defend our right to be here, wanted or not. The child who is not helped in this is forced to bend or sacrifice in ways that can be crippling to the self-image, crushing self-worth. Symbolically healing or defending such a picture is going to give the child reinforcement and let them know they do have rights.

DISCUSSION STARTERS

Do you ever feel like this tree?
What other solutions can you think up to help this tree?
Do you know people who act like the tractor?
What happens when you tell people they are hurting your feelings?

Carlos (10)

The Spanish Skeleton

84

[Carlos was born in Puerto Rico. His ancestors were Spanish. He has been at school in the United States for three years.]

I dream that I am up in my room and the globe on my bookcase looks like a dead head. I walk downstairs to get a cup of milk, but there is a skeleton chained to the wall near the refrigerator. I am so scared I wake up shaking.

CARLOS'S SOLUTION

I drew my dream. Then I closed my eyes and stepped back into the dream. I couldn't talk to the skeleton; he was too scary until I put some clothes on him. I dressed him in Yankee things like Robin Hood and Peter Pan. Then I could talk to him. I asked him what he's doing in my dream. He says he's been locked up and my house was the dungeon. He said, "Hey thanks for dressing me American. Now I feel peppy. Cut me loose." I cut the lock and set him free. He says he comes from the old country, but he wants to be American now, not a deadhead. And that feels better to be dressed Yankee.

DIALOGUE

Guide: Close your eyes again. What do you see?

Carlos: Oh, yes he's there alright, chained to the wall.

Guide: Do you feel safe enough to ask him what he wants?

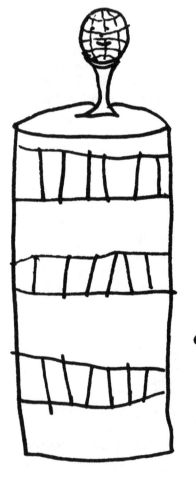

Carlos: He's watching me get a cup of milk. He doesn't say anything. He just stares at me. Now I'm scared.

Guide: Back off and make yourself safe. How will you make it less scary?

Carlos: Unhook him. Dress him up in Yankee clothes right over his old bones. There, it's done. . . . He looks like Peter Pan with a Robin Hood hat on. . . .[Carlos draws in a Robin Hood hat.] He says he feels peppy.

Guide: Ask him why he came into your dream.

Carlos: He wants to be released. He was locked up by some old king for centuries. He says my house was the old dungeon.

Guide: So you've released the old skeleton. . . . How does that feel?

Carlos: Yeah. He is glad I let him free. Glad I wasn't a deadhead. Glad I had courage like Robin Hood. Glad I believed in him like Peter Pan. Now he can get smart. I feel better.

COMMENTS

Satisfaction came quickly, as though all Carlos needed was affirmation and the symbolic act to move along. It can be very difficult for a child to grow up in two cultures simultaneously. It is not always easy to make a bridge between the old and the new, particularly if it involves different traditions and values and a new school with different attitudes. Children are often confused or ashamed by old family customs, confusing their fidelity to old and new. Frequently children from Third World cultures accept the prejudicial expectations that are categorically leveled at them by the new world, with the result that they see themselves as inadequate or less than bright. We need to help them understand this problem.

85

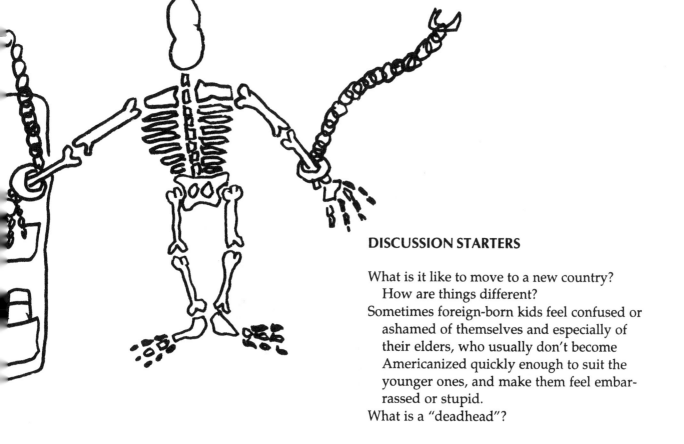

DISCUSSION STARTERS

What is it like to move to a new country? How are things different?

Sometimes foreign-born kids feel confused or ashamed of themselves and especially of their elders, who usually don't become Americanized quickly enough to suit the younger ones, and make them feel embarrassed or stupid.

What is a "deadhead"?

Molly (5)

My House Was on Fire

I dreamed my house was on fire. I was inside, and so was my cat. My dad was at the office. My mom was at the store. I woke up screaming, "Help! Help! I'm going to burn up!" I woke up so scared I was petrified. I thought my cat and I would wake up dead.

MOLLY'S SOLUTION

I drew my dream, but I didn't like seeing me burning up inside the house, so I had to get out. I drew myself out on the street, but I'm not allowed to cross the street. So I drew in a policeman to help. He took me across the street. Then I could run to the shop to get my mother. But the doorknob was too high to open the door. So I had to get a box to stand on. Then I opened the door and ran upstairs to tell my mom. Together we got the fireman to put the fire out and they saved my cat. When I got home from the dream workshop, I showed my picture to my mom and we decided it was time to have a fire drill like they do at school, in case of emergency. I can think for myself.

DIALOGUE

Guide: What is that little face in the window saying?

Molly: HELP HELP!!! It's really scary to be inside a burning house. I'm scared to look at the picture.

Guide: How will you save that little girl in the picture?

Molly: I'll have to get her out of the house, even though she's not allowed when mom and dad are out.

Guide: Good idea. Can you draw yourself outside of the house?

Molly: Yes, I'm on the street, but I can't do anything.

Guide: Why not?

Molly: Because I'm not allowed to cross the street, and my mom is across the street at the store.

Guide: What are you going to do? . . . It certainly looks like an emergency, Molly. What are you allowed to do in an emergency? Isn't your cat still inside?

Molly: I could find someone . . . maybe a policeman. I'll draw a policeman. He can cross me.

Guide: I see you can think for yourself. Then what?

Molly: Now I can run and get my mom in the store.

Guide: Close your eyes and see yourself doing that. What do you see?

Molly: I see that I can't get in the store.

Guide: Why not?

Molly: Because the doorknob is too high for me to reach.

Guide: What will you do? Close your eyes and see yourself reaching the door knob.... How did you do it?

Molly: I got a box to stand on.

Guide: Good idea. . . . Draw it in.

Molly: It worked. I got a box and opened the door. I found my mom. . . . She was upstairs. [Molly writes "Hi, Mom" into her picture.]

Guide: Now what? Is that the end?

Molly: My cat is in the house. Mommy! Mommy! Call the fireman! The house is on fire and the cat will burn up! Quick! Quick!

Guide: It looks like you're not so helpless as you thought. How do you dial help?

COMMENTS

Some children are very literal. It is a form of protection. If you follow instructions to the letter of the law, you think yourself blame-free. That's why house rules can be even stronger than common sense. Most children try to be good, and feel guilty when they break the house rules. If they are brought up to do what they're told, children have a hard time switching into self-motivated gear. They lack permission to think for themselves; they wait for permission and direction. (We trained them from birth after all!) Molly's nightmare shows us that this situation can be very dangerous in the event of an emergency, or when she is left alone with instructions not to leave the house, not to cross the street, not to speak to strangers. At age five, when children are sent out of our care into situations where they have to think for themselves, they may need permission to use their own judgment to save themselves. (Up until now, it was better for Molly to "be good" than to think for herself—but some part of her feared the consequences. This nightmare was a good warning.)

Dreams about fires might be a signal that a child needs to talk over emergency procedures or to rehearse a fire drill at home. In order to free children of the need for approval and outside direction, we need to help them test their own judgment and learn to trust their own wisdom. To do this, we need to lift any parental prohibitions which are no longer workable. Many parents and teachers have trouble with this: they prefer docile obedience. This may make life easier for the adult, but the child pays a big price in the end. It restricts the development of self-confidence and the understanding of the relationship between cause and effect upon which independence and confidence are built. (Incidentally, this dream work helps children who "escape" from fear by hiding under the bed or pulling the covers over their heads. Check it out. Empowerment, even if only symbolic, is like a rehearsal. Once new information is in the inner computer, attitudes and behavior will change.)

DISCUSSION STARTERS

In case of fire, what should you do?
Have you ever had an emergency that you had to handle yourself?
If your house was burning, would you hide in the closet?

Kelly (10)

The Baby-Sitter's Nightmare

I often dream that I am baby-sitting for my sister, who is five. Just me and the television. Some bad man comes into the house and I am so scared I don't know what to do.

KELLY'S SOLUTION

I made a list of all the telephone numbers I might need in case of trouble, like: how to call the police, how to call the fire department, how to call a neighbor who would be home if I had a question, the telephone number of where my parents are if I got scared from watching a TV show.

I AM SO SCARED I DON'T KNOW WHAT TO DO.

COMMENTS

Many of us trust our children's competence to such an extent that we burden them with responsibilities far too big for them to carry comfortably. They may worry about all the terrible things, real and imaginary, that could happen while they are in charge. They may not be able to tell us of their fears because they need adult approval more than they need their own self-respect. One solution would be to lighten the child's load of responsibilities; another is to help the child prepare for the real problems that could arise when they are in charge.

DISCUSSION STARTERS

In case of emergency, what help is available to you? Make your list and ask your parents for their emergency list.

You seem so dependable and intelligent that grown-ups may forget that you are still a child. How can you discuss this with them?

Do you feel comfortable with the responsibilities you are asked to carry?

It's better not to watch scary movies or television shows when you are alone with big responsibilities like baby-sitting.

The Toilet Paper Wizard

I was walking in a cave with my father. I walked until I came to the end of the tunnel. I saw a light and a lake and then I saw a stair. I walked up and up until I saw a giant roll of toilet paper. I tried to pull it down. The more I pulled, the more it pulled me up. My father called me, but I said, "No. You come up here. There is a giant roll of toilet paper and it's pulling me up." Father said, "OK, I'll come and pull it down," but he too got pulled up. Then I woke up. It felt scary to be alone in that cave with my father.

JULIET'S SOLUTION

I went back into that tunnel and talked to the giant roll of toilet paper and the King of Toilet Wizard and to the black bat with the yellow eyes. I couldn't get the toilet paper to let me go. It was protecting me from the dark and the unknown. I needed it to protect me until I got some light that I could control. After working on this dream, I asked my dad to buy me a flashlight so I could pick myself up at night and light my way to the toilet in the dark by myself. Then the toilet paper let go of me, and I wasn't so scared as I thought. I felt brave to take charge of the Toilet Paper Wizard.

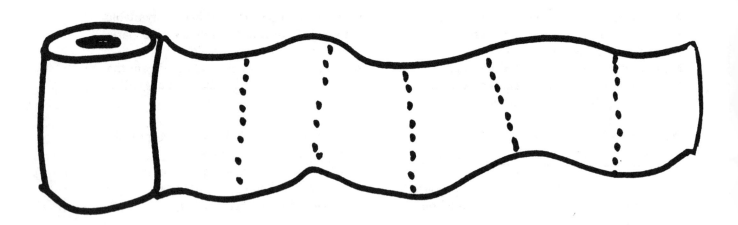

DIALOGUE

[This dialogue was lengthy because we didn't understand at first how important the giant roll was.]

Guide: What would have made you feel safer?

Juliet: If we'd been with someone who knew the way, someone who could talk and communicate with people.

Guide: If you could communicate what would you say?

Juliet: I'd find a creature—a weird creature I'd never seen before—a wizard who knew the place.

Guide: What help would he give you?

Juliet: He'd show me the way out.

Guide: You want to get out. What does your father say?

Juliet: I don't know what my father says.

Guide: Close your eyes and go back into the tunnel. What do you see?

Juliet: I see my father. He is always walking slowly. He walks behind me. He goes on down the tunnel.

Guide: Then what?

Juliet: He picks me up.

Guide: How does that feel?

Juliet: There is a scary black bat with yellow eyes. We're afraid of him.

Guide: Shall we talk to the scary bat or the toilet paper roll who won't let go?

Juliet: The toilet paper keeps pulling me up. It won't let me down.

Guide: How do you think paper can be so strong?

Juliet: It looks like ordinary toilet paper but it isn't.

Guide: It seems to have a lot of power over you. What would you like to say or do to it?

Juliet: I could try to make it smaller.

Guide: Try that.

Juliet: It just got larger and stronger—like a mad scientist was doing some strange things to it. I couldn't pull it apart. It won't rip.

Guide: Close your eyes and see what you need to be in charge of this situation?

Juliet: I need to make it smaller. I could go back in the cave if my father would let me and get one of those torches and try to burn it.

Guide: Try that.

Juliet: My father won't let me.

Guide: Why not?

Juliet: He thinks there is something back in the dark cave that will get me.

Guide: Can you think of another way?

Juliet: I might go up the stairs, but there might be something up there, too, that would get me.

Guide: What do you need?

Juliet: I need some light . . . but it still pulls me up, even when it's lighter and lighter up there.

Guide: Try another solution.

Juliet: Maybe I could let go.

Guide: Try that.

Juliet: But I fell back.

Guide: Could you make something soft to land on?

Juliet: No, my father could catch me, but now he won't go down again, so we have to follow the toilet paper into the dark part.

Guide: Follow the toilet paper. Where does it end?

Juliet: [Silently she follows.] I follow and follow. . . . It takes me all over the place in the dark. I can't see where it wants to take me.

Guide: Where do you want it to take you?

Juliet: To the end—where the light gets brighter. But all I see are more and more rolls of paper pushing me back into the tunnel.

Guide: What would help? Close your eyes and see yourself getting to the light.

Juliet: I need something to cut through it. I can't find anything. . . . All I can think to do now is talk to the King of the Toilet.

Guide: Try that.

Juliet: All it did was roll around. At the end of the tube I see red eyes and a mouth.

Guide: Can you talk to it?

Juliet: It says to stop bothering it. It thinks we are the enemy.

Guide: Ask it what it wants.

I was walking in a cave
with my fother I walkde and
walkde

94

in tall I came to the end
of the tunill
I saw
a la ke.
and then I saw a ster
and I walkde up and up the ster
tall I saw
gicint
role of tolat paeper

Juliet: It wants to see what is in our pockets. All I found was a yo-yo and a rubber ball. In my back pocket I had five dollars and two cents. It says I wouldn't know where to go if I got past it.

Guide: Say that last part again: You wouldn't know where to go if you passed it?

Juliet: That's what it said. . . .

Guide: It might be a new sort of freedom if the toilet paper let you go by. You might be in charge of yourself. You wouldn't need your father walking in the dark.

Juliet: I'm afraid because I don't know what's out there. If I get past it, it might be a trap. Something inside me says, "No, you might get caught."

Guide: It sounds like you need a guide. Can you create a guide? You know you can always create a guide when no one is around to help.

Juliet: OK. I've got my guide now. My guide took me back to see what is there in the cave. We saw a big green monster. My guide asks him if we can go by. The monster answers in a funny language I don't understand.

Guide: Ask the guide what you want to know.

Juliet: I want to know the answer to this mystery. I'd like to know it won't come after me if I go past it. My guide says the monster should let me go by, so he let me go by. Now he is behind me instead of in front of me.

Guide: How does that feel?

Juliet: Now I don't know what is in front of me.

Guide: What would help?

Juliet: I'd like to rip it off now.

Guide: Try that.

Juliet: I did try, but I can't see what is in front of me because the toilet paper roll is still there. It's very big. . . . It keeps everything away. . . . It wouldn't be safe to make it smaller. It's used to being in front. . . . If it's smaller it won't protect me.

Guide: It protects you from what?

Juliet: It's used to seeing the things in front but I'm not. It has met what's in front and I never have.

Guide: It sounds like you need that roll of toilet paper to hide behind.

Juliet: I guess so. It is scarier without it.

Guide: Ask how long before you'll get the courage to let it stop protecting you.

Juliet: It says soon but not now. First I have to go back home. Then I will come back another day.

Guide: Maybe by then you'll ask your dad to give you a flashlight so you can pick yourself up and take yourself to the toilet at night. Then you can see what's in front of you in the dark. Then you will be in charge of the Toilet Paper Wizard instead of letting him be in charge of you.

95

COMMENTS

We have probably all had a fear of the dark at one time or another in our lives. Some children are so afraid of the dark that getting to the bathroom at night presents a problem. It helps for children to talk about their fears with someone who feels sympathetic. It is not helpful to mock their fears, or add our fears to theirs if we can help it. When parents are afraid for their children, it tends to intensify the children's fears, and make it almost impossible for them to find the courage to try new things. On the other hand, somtimes keeping parents worried is a child's only way to have their attention, in which case it's hard to give it up. Sometimes parents use the child to help them face their own fears or loneliness. That is a bond that is very hard to break.

DISCUSSION STARTERS

Do your parents worry about you too much?
Are they afraid for your safety?
Do you like to worry them?
If you pick yourself up at night, would you lose your dad or mom's attention?

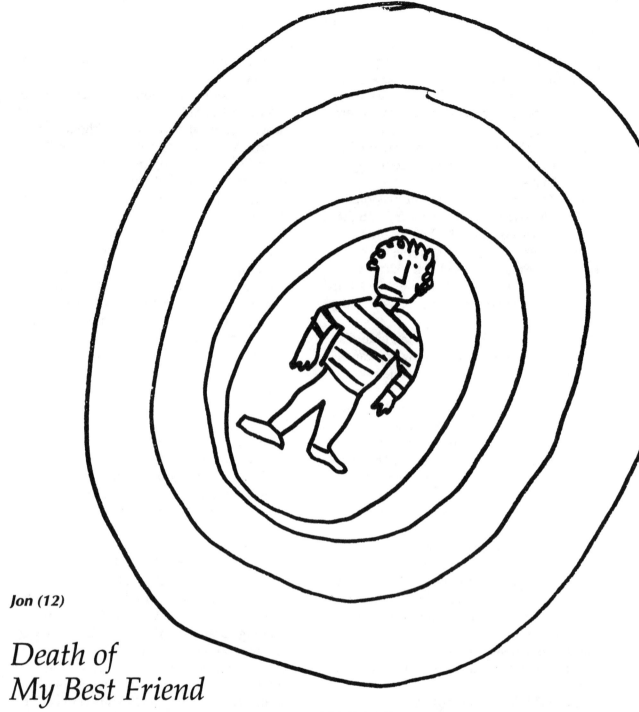

Jon (12)

Death of My Best Friend

I was at camp. I dreamed I was in this big tunnel. It made me afraid someone was going to die. I thought it was me. Later my dream came true. It was my best friend that died. He was nice to me. I taught him commands. When I went away to camp, he wouldn't eat. My mother said he died from missing me. I was so important, he died of a broken heart. My best friend was my lizard.

JON'S SOLUTION

When my mother wrote me at camp to tell me that my best friend died, I felt like crying. It was just like the bad dream. At first I didn't want to see him dead, but after I drew him alive, I asked the picture to talk. I told him that boys have to go to camp to learn new things, and lizards don't live as long as people do. I told him we had a good life together and he was my best friend. He said he understood and forgives me. He said he could lead me out of the dark tunnel, and he did.

DIALOGUE

Guide: When you look at the picture, what does that make you feel?

Jon: Sad. I didn't realize a person like me could be that important and I'm trapped in that tunnel. . . . Helpless.

Guide: It's a big responsibility to have the life of someone or a pet depend on you, especially when you feel trapped.

Jon: I didn't do it on purpose. My mom wanted me to go to camp and I have to stay now.

Guide: That kind of situation is a kind of a trap, isn't it?

Jon: Yes, and it made me want to go home. I felt so homesick that maybe I could die of a broken heart, too.

Guide: If you could talk to the lizard, what do you think it would say?

Jon: He'd say you're the best friend I ever had and now I don't have any.

Guide: What would make it feel better?

Jon: If my mother hadn't said it died from missing me.

Guide: What can you imagine that would make it right between you and your lizard? What would you say? And what would the lizard say?

Jon: I'd say, "I'm sorry, and thank you for being my friend," and he'd say, "I know you didn't mean to break my heart."

COMMENTS

It's wonderful to have pets and putting children in charge of one is a good way to help them understand responsibility, but too often it ends in heavy feelings of guilt or entrapment if they did not ask for the pet or if they are not old enough to undertake full responsibility. We forget sometimes that children are apt to take things literally (to die of a broken heart) and that they are quick to think they are the cause when things go wrong. Some of the worst stuck places in psychotherapy are built on these kinds of childhood assumptions.

DISCUSSION STARTERS

Can people die of a broken heart?
Have you ever lost a pet you loved?
Do you know how long different kinds of animals live?
Do you know what a double bind is?
How is Jon caught in a double bind? [His mother makes him leave his lizard and go to camp and then tells him his friend the lizard died from missing him.]

Judy (35)

It's No Joke

I am walking to Granny's house. There is a hairy gorilla waiting in the trees. He jumps out and grabs me in his arms. He carries me to my father who I thought would save me. Instead, my father tells the monster not to worry. He said, "My daughter won't hurt you." Then the gorilla said, "It's nothing personal, I'm just doing my job." I had this dream many times between the ages of seven and eleven, and never forgave my father, until I worked on this dream twenty-eight years later.

JUDY'S SOLUTION

I felt betrayed and angry to think that my father would defend the gorilla instead of his daughter. For twenty-eight years I couldn't forgive him until I drew my dream and stepped back inside the little girl. This is what I hear her say: "Since you won't defend me, Father, I'll defend myself. Put my baby girl down this minute, you big gorilla. And as for you, Father, it's no joke, to be grabbed by a stranger and frightened while your father laughs at you telling the stranger that a child won't hurt him. For twenty-eight years I've felt hurt and betrayed. I never found your sarcasm amusing. I have not been able to forgive your insensitivity."

COMMENTS

It is often beneficial for adults to work out nightmares that haunted them as children. Judy worked out a solution to her childhood nightmare years after it ceased to visit her. She showed the picture to her father, who had never realized how sensitive little kids can be about such things. He apologized to her twenty-eight years late, nevertheless it put an end to a bothersome episode in her life, and erased a stuck memory. Judy's dream clearly demonstrates that making a child the butt of a joke can cause deep and lasting feelings of rejection. Sarcasm is one of the hardest things for children to understand, especially if it feels like a betrayal of innocence.

DISCUSSION STARTERS

What does it feel like when people are laughing at you?

What can you do?

Can you tell them you feel hurt?

It's best to settle things when they are fresh instead of waiting twenty-eight years.

Nina (10)

The Alligator's Revenge

I am riding in a canoe with a friend—but it's also my father. They are both in my dream. I just remember falling out of the boat and this alligator came to eat me. This is me screaming, "Help!" I know he is coming to eat off my legs, and the canoe is too far to swim to. He can eat me even on the land. I can't get away. This alligator was the king of all alligators. To get safe, I hid in the top of a tree. When I asked him why he wanted to eat me he said "'Cause your father killed my wife."

You see, my father is an importer; he has to kill alligators for their skins, and my class is studying endangered animals. So when I had this dream, I was very scared there was no place to hide because he had the right to kill me because it's against the law to kill alligators and my father killed his wife.

NINA'S SOLUTION

This picture really scares me. The only place the alligator can't reach is the top of a palm tree, so I drew myself up in a tree. I told the king of the alligators I was really sorry but it wasn't my fault. He said he'd give me one more chance. I promised to talk to my father and suggest we sell plants instead of killing animals. Probably my father won't listen, but at least the alligator won't blame me.

DIALOGUE

Guide: Your father killed his wife?

Nina: Yes, my father kills alligators for their skins, so the alligator was furious at me and everything. He wanted to rip me apart and eat me up. There was no hiding place, he is King of the Jungle.

Guide: How are you going to help the girl in your picture?

Nina: I don't know.

Guide: You are certainly in a difficult spot. Try something.

Nina: Well, I would like to tie him up and contact the canoe.

Guide: How will you do that?

Nina: Yell "HELP." [Writes in "HELP" on her drawing.]

Guide: That's a start. What's next?

Nina: I'll start to swim, but the canoe is too far away. I think I'm going to swim to land instead. It's nearer . . . but these birds are mean. He's KING of everything, even King of the birds, 'cause alligators can go on land, too. I can hide up in a tree and try to convince the alligator that I won't hurt him if he won't hurt me.

Guide: How are you doing that?

Nina: I'm talking to him. He says, "NO way. You've killed my wife and I'm going to kill you," and I said, "I didn't kill your wife, my daddy did." Alligator says, "Well OK, I'll give you one more chance." I guess that's why I'm still alive.

Guide: It must feel bad to be blamed for your father's actions, and even harder to tell on him.

Nina: That's it.

Guide: Does that happen often to you?

Nina: Sometimes . . . yeah.

Guide: Tell the alligator about it.

Nina: Well, sometimes my class blames me. We get in arguments about things they think we do—something bad—and we really don't. Now the alligator begins to like me a little . . . but I'd still feel better in the canoe. He knows I'm really sorry about killing endangered animals.

Guide: How did it happen?

Nina: Well, I overheard my father say about going to get a king-sized alligator in the Everglades for a lot of money for someone like a king. So he went out and caught it. He didn't realize it was the alligator's wife.

Guide: Do you talk about killing animals for their skins in class?

Nina: Well, yes, and he didn't mean to kill the wife. . . . He did mean to kill the animal for a lot of money. Yes, they make pocketbooks . . . very expensive ones.

Guide: Close your eyes and bring your father into the picture. Talk with him.

Nina: I'll ask him why he did it. . . . He says he has to earn a living to feed us kids. If I use my imagination I'll ask him to make a potion to make the alligator come back to life. He says he'll try, but it won't work.

Guide: Hum.

102

Nina: He's giving the potion to her. . . . Her eyes open. . . . She says, "Where am I?" I say, "You're at my house." She says, "Where is your house?" "A long way from here, but I'll take you home." I say, "Daddy, can we bring her home?" He says, "Yes," so now I am clean. I'm back home. It's all right.

Guide: So you resuscitated the dead alligator and explained your innocence. Anything you want to say to your father?

Nina: Don't kill anything. Let's take a plant and sell that. Don't ever kill an alligator again.

COMMENTS

In their contacts outside the home—with friends, school, church, TV—children are exposed to a variety of value systems that are often inconsistent with home practices. The dilemma is particularly uncomfortable when social standards come in conflict with what is practiced or preached by the breadwinner. Children often feel confused and guilty when they come to believe their parents are acting immorally. At the same time, they may feel compelled to defend their parents' actions, which leads to further confusion and guilt. Understanding the source of the conflict and talking it out with a sympathetic listener should be helpful.

DISCUSSION STARTERS

How does it feel to be blamed for your parents' actions? Values change from generation to generation. Fur coats and animal skins used to be popular. Now ecologists tell us we have endangered many species for the sake of their skins, and they beg us to stop before the animals are all gone forever from this earth. But what if our parents make a living in a job that requires killing these animals? What do we do then?

There are other jobs that could cause this kind of conflict, for instance jobs dealing with military defense, nuclear weapons, experimenting on animals, selling food in foam containers, or jobs where you use aerosol sprays. Can you think of any others?

We and the children of the new age have serious decisions to make about how we treat the creatures of this earth, and no time to lose.

Dale (22)

The Pedestal Dream

I had this dream throughout my childhood. I dreamed I am standing on a high pedestal in the middle of the Roman Colosseum waiting to be thrown to the lions about to enter the arena. Then water starts to pour into the place and it fills up within ten feet of me. Then the pillar cracks, plunging me into the whirlpool which sucks me in, so I wake suffocating for air.

DALE'S SOLUTION

By drawing a lion tamer to distract the lions, and a helicopter to bring a ladder, I've rescued that poor kid at last. I also realized that I had not climbed up onto that pedestal, so maybe I was born there or put there by other people's expectations. I decided to lower the expectations to a more comfortable height, something I can handle, and avoid the lion's den that can suck me in over my head. I've been dreaming this dream for twenty years. Now that I've solved it, I don't expect this dream will come back again.

COMMENTS

Sometimes dreams show us stuck in high places and we don't know how we got there. It may mean that we are trying to live up to expectations, our own or our parents', that are too high. Parental expectations are especially hard to live up to.

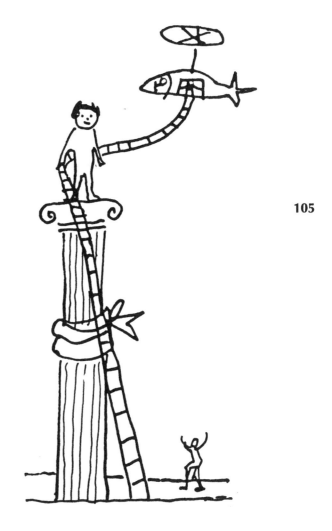

DISCUSSION STARTERS

Do you have expectations that seem too high? How can you modify them?

Can you find a metaphor in this dream [being thrown to the lions, getting sucked in, feeling in over your head, put on a pedestal, etc.]? There are lots of metaphor in dreams. Learn to recognize them.

Marko (11)

The Hanging Man

106 I dreamed that a bad man burst through my door and accused me of terrible things I hadn't done. He said he would hang me by my toes until I was dead. I was so scared I woke up and found myself on the floor under my bed, my heart pounding so I could hardly breathe.

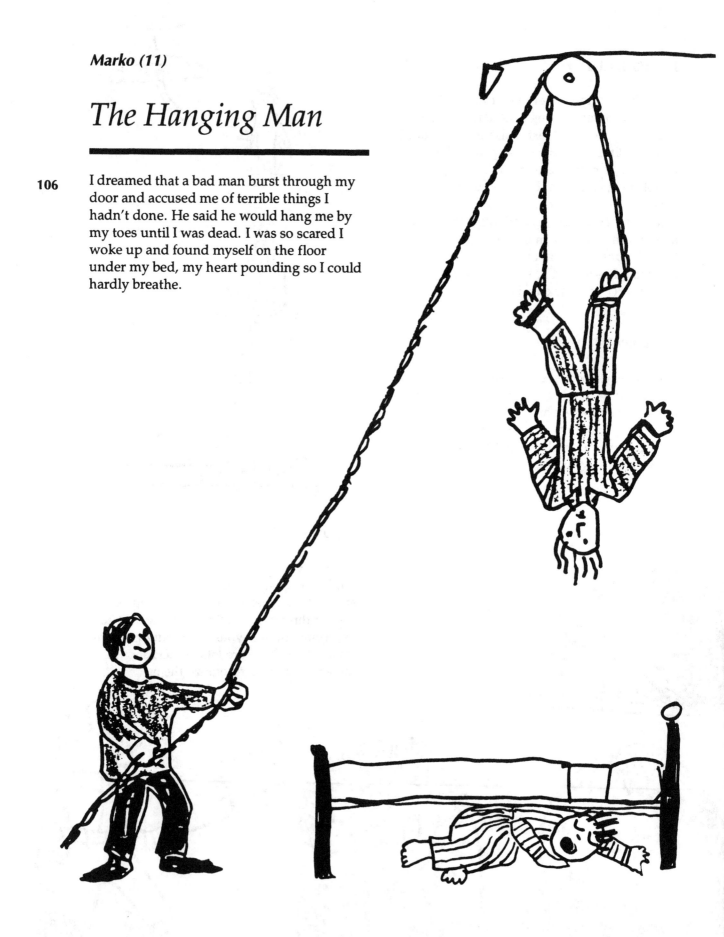

MARKO'S SOLUTION

I drew this dream, closed my eyes, stepped back into the scene, and got some help. What I need is a lawyer who believes I'm innocent, and a court of law to hear my case. So I drew it into the picture. The bad man had to let me down since, according to American law, everyone has a right to a fair trial. The message is about how I feel when I'm accused and I'm innocent. I feel as helpless as a man hanging by his toes. Next time I feel like that in real life, I'll use that lawyer I found inside myself. It's better than crying for help under the bed.

COMMENTS

Children often feel they have been unfairly treated or unjustly accused by the adults who care for them. If they have no way to "plead their case," they feel helpless, stuck. As adults, we need to allow children some recourse in case we are wrong or have misunderstood them. I find that kids, in general, are basically honest, according to their own point of view and logic. We all have wisdom that lives inside us which we have not yet learned to use. Dreams often challenge us to confront our helplessness and find a way out of a tough situation creatively, instead of waiting to be rescued.

DISCUSSION STARTERS

Have you ever felt unjustly accused?
What does it mean to have your "day in court"?
What would help better than hiding under the bed?

Afterword

As I reread this manuscript, I am struck by the emergencies children live with in silence. I think if it were not for this pilot dream workshop, these young people might never have aired their complex dilemmas. And this is just a mild example of the concerns children have.

When I took this workshop to a Boston public school to supervise one of my students, the nightmares the children discussed posed many sexually focused problems. A thirteen-year-old girl dreamed that her sister was raped and dumped in the alley beside their house. This initiated a lively discussion about what to do if your sister was captive; what to do if rape and incest were taking place right under your nose. Who to call? Who to tell? What if you were next on the list?

By next morning, we were in trouble. Parents had called the principal to find out why rape was being discussed in the afternoon art program. Why were we teaching their children the horrors of life? We were asked to close our dream-drawing project, and all the fears were returned to silence.

My passion for this work stems from the revelation that we do to ourselves and to others the things that were done to us, unless we find a way to break the cycle. Transformation and creativity are two of the most healing aspects of this work. What we cannot change, we can reframe; what we cannot undo, we can transform. The power of suggestion is sometimes all that is needed to stimulate change: stepping outside of a problem, reversing roles, listening to both sides, becoming the conscious observer. And creativity is the best and the fastest healer.

But why wait to make these changes? Why not teach positive survival strategies to young children so that respect for their self-worth becomes part of their basic structure? How can we go on teaching kids the abstract disciplines of mathematics, grammar, and science, and neglect the realities that cripple their survival and threaten their security and growth?

After working in the creative arts and expressive therapies for twenty and more years, I am still amazed at how many people have had their creativity crushed by the time they are seven or eight years old. I believe creativity is innate in us all, and that expressing it is our birthright. But if it is unvalued in the school and in the home in favor of obedience and programmed learning, it shrivels like a weed at the edge of the trodden path.

As parents, teachers, and therapists, we are in the position to give young people permission to bloom in the positive light of self-worth and to transfrom negative survival strategies into creative assets. This is a very priviliged and exciting role to play. It is how we live on into the future.

CPSIA information can be obtained
at www.ICGtesting.com
Printed in the USA
BVHW010917151020
591111BV00013B/232